Denaby & Cadeby Main Collieries

The Development of a Mining Community

Dave Fordham

Acknowledgements

The author would like to thank the following for their assistance in compiling this work: Peter Bagshawe, Brian Brownsword, Keith Butcher, S. J Butler, Dave Careless, Barrie Dolby, Noman Ellis, Richard Fordham, John Fordham, Paul Fox, Dave Heywood, Mel Jones, Julie Knight, John Law, Andrew McGarrigle, Peter Mitchell, Carol Narey, David Packer, John Petch, Jim Reeves, John Ryan, Joan Ulley, Geoff Warnes, and the staff of Doncaster Archives, Rotherham Archives and Sheffield Archives. Acknowledgment is also extended to Doncaster Local Studies Library for allowing access to contemporary newspaper records from *The Doncaster Gazette* and *The Doncaster Chronicle;* the University of Birmingham Library for viewing their copies of *The Colliery Guardian*; and the Conisbrough & Denaby Main Heritage Group for their help and assistance. Finally, I acknowledge a debt to the early postcard photographers whose work has been used to illustrate this publication, in particular Walter Roelich, Edgar Scrivens, R. J. Rossor and James Simonton & Sons. Every effort has been made to attribute copyright to the illustrations used in this publication, although it has proved impossible to determine who drew the housing block plans reproduced from Doncaster Archives - anyone who asserts copyright over these plans is asked to contact the author and Doncaster Archives. Unless otherwise credited, all illustrations featured in this publication are from the author's collection and all attempts to attribute copyright have been made.

Published by Fedj-el-Adoum Publishing
3 Adelaide Road, Norton, Doncaster, South Yorkshire, DN6 9EW

© Fedj-el-Adoum Publishing & Dave Fordham 2016

ISBN 978-09562864-6-8

First Edition 2016

All rights reserved. No part of this publication may be reproduced, stored in a retrieval system, or transmitted, in any form or by any means, electronic, mechanical, photocopying, recording, or otherwise without written permission of the author.

Cover Illustration

Denaby Main Colliery as recorded by local postcard publisher Edgar Scrivens in the early 1930s. This view features the newly reconstructed No. 2 headgear and the large railway signal box that controlled the level crossing and access to the various sidings. This photograph was captured from a position above the cliffs of a small quarry and a comparative view can be seen today by pedestrians walking along the northern side of Bambury Bridge. (Brian Brownsword Collection).

Denaby & Cadeby Main Collieries

The Development of a Mining Community

Frontispiece: *This terrific colour photograph captures a quiet Sunday morning in Denaby Main in 1965 and was taken from the footbridge that spanned the railway. Today, every building visible in this picture of Doncaster Road has been demolished. However, the milestone remains, having survived the coming of the colliery in 1863 and having been passed by numerous 'Denabyites' every day up to the closure of the pit in 1968. (John Law Collection).*

Cadeby Main Colliery from the River Don

This is one of several attractive water colours (possibly produced by C. V. Clarke) used to illustrate the publication 'Modern Methods of Coal Production and Shipment', published by Yorkshire Amalgamated Collieries c.1928. It depicts a stylised view of Cadeby Main Colliery complete with passing barge and railway wagons from the various colliery undertakings which merged to form Yorkshire Amalgamated Collieries in 1927. (Yorkshire Amalgamated Collieries - Author Collection).

Denaby & Cadeby Main Collieries

"In that pleasant district of merry England which is watered by the River Don, there extended in ancient times a large forest, covering the greater part of the beautiful hills and valleys which lie between Sheffield and the pleasant town of Doncaster." – Sir Walter Scott, 1820.

When Sir Walter Scott wrote the above lines which open his novel *Ivanhoe,* set in the area around Conisbrough Castle, his 'pleasant district of merry England' was already being affected by the onslaught of industrialisation, albeit on a very small scale, as below the castle on the banks of the River Don, ironmasters Samuel and Aaron Walker of Rotherham had established the Burcroft Boring Mills in 1779 for the manufacture of cannon balls. However, apart from this small industrial incursion, the region was dominated by agriculture and had a very pleasing rural aspect with fields, meadows, woods and rocky crags. Standing on top of the magnificent castle keep in 1820, Sir Walter Scott would have surveyed a picturesque scene.

The Castle was strategically placed atop a rocky hill guarding the entrance to the Don Gorge where the River Don, having collected the waters of the River Dearne at Denaby and a small brook at Burcroft, had eroded a deep and narrow valley through the prominent limestone escarpment towards the east. To the south lies the small mediaeval settlement of Conisbrough (originally Conisborough) which had largely developed to service the castle, although its origins pre-date the construction of the castle on account of its church, dedicated to St Peter, which dates back to Saxon times. The northerly view is dominated by the limestone escarpment with its hilltop villages of Cadeby and High Melton. The steep western-facing slope of the escarpment overlooks the low lying agricultural lands and flood plain meadows adjoining the old hamlet of Denaby, a settlement of farms and cottages within the Parish of Mexborough and forming part of the Denaby estate owned by Sir John Reresby and later by John Fullerton of Thrybergh Hall. Beyond Denaby is the larger settlement of Mexborough on the northern bank of the River Don. At this time, the population of Conisbrough was larger than Mexborough. However, the latter settlement was undergoing industrialisation and by the time of the 1861 census the population of Mexborough at 2,462 had exceeded that of Conisbrough which numbered 1,655.

Construction of the great fortress at Conisbrough, located approximately 7 miles to the west of Doncaster and 16 miles to the north-east of Sheffield, had begun in 1159 by Hamelin Plantagenet, half-brother of King Henry II. Hamelin Plantagenet had married Isabel Warenne, the great granddaughter of William de Warenne who had been granted the manor of Conisbrough following the Norman Conquest in 1066. This postcard, published by Edgar Scrivens in 1924, shows the splendid hexagonal keep with the tower of St Peter's Church in Conisbrough to the left. The view is taken from the crags on Minney Moor, a natural rock outcrop forming the eroded remnants of a coral reef within the Magnesian Limestone that lies above the Coal Measures strata in this area.

Thus by 1861, the 203 inhabitants of Denaby were largely unaccustomed to the effects of industrialisation, most of the population working off the land and for the tenanted farms of the settlement. However, they would have been accustomed to coal mining as their fields were situated upon rocks belonging to the Coal Measures which form the 'exposed coalfield' of South Yorkshire, so called because the coal bearing strata are exposed at the surface. Despite their name, the Coal Measures, extending for a depth of 1,500 yards beneath Denaby, are not actually dominated by coal but comprise a series of alternating layers of sandstones, shales and clays together with occasional coal seams. Paramount amongst these is the 10 feet thick 'Barnsley Bed'. This seam is named after the town of Barnsley some 12 miles to the north-west where it comes to the surface.

The Coal Measures rocks are gently inclined to the east so that, as one progresses in an easterly direction from Barnsley to Denaby, the coal seams lie at increasing depths. From Denaby to Doncaster the easterly inclination of the strata continues and the Coal Measures are buried beneath a cover of younger rocks which form the limestone escarpment that overlooks Mexborough, Denaby and Conisbrough.

This limestone, traditionally referred to as the Magnesian Limestone, now has the scientific name Cadeby Formation, due to its exposure in the quarries near Cadeby. As the Coal Measures rocks are now no longer exposed at the surface, hidden from view by a cover of younger rocks, this part of the South Yorkshire coalfield has become known as the 'concealed coalfield'.

Old Denaby as seen from the track leading to the ferry across the River Don to Mexborough Church. Despite the fact that during the first 30 years of the 20th Century the number of people living in the mining communities around Doncaster had increased from 27,865 to 156,187, Old Denaby remains a quiet and rural enclave. Originally known simply as Denaby, it acquired the prefix 'Old' around 1870 to distinguish it from the new settlement adjacent to the colliery which was referred to as Denaby Main. This postcard by Edgar Scrivens dates from 1930.

The earliest record of coal mining in the Denaby area dates to a deed of 1487 mentioning a field named as 'Colepytes' and old Ordnance Survey maps of the area show an area of woodland named Coal Pit Plantation. During the 17th and early 18th Centuries, small-scale coal extraction was active from the shallow Shafton coal seam and in 1766, William Cartright was mining this seam from a 45 feet deep shaft adjacent to Denaby Woods. Coal from this and other small pits in the area was transported along wooden wagon-ways to the River Don, which had been made navigable to traffic from 1751. To the west of Denaby not far from the River Don is Engine House Farm, its name arising from another small-scale venture employing a steam engine to raise coal from the Shafton coal seam.

In the 1850s, a consortium led by Joseph Thornton of Southgate in Middlesex, and the Waring Brothers (John Waring of Conisbrough, Thomas Waring of Swinton and Joseph Waring of Braithwell), approached the Fullerton family in order to secure a coal lease beneath the Denaby estate. Joseph Thornton was born in Snaith near Goole in 1804 but was resident at Beaver Hall in Southgate and the Waring brothers were farmers and minor landowners looking to diversify their interests into coal mining. Early records are somewhat unclear but it appears that this syndicate made a series of test bores and even commenced work on an unsuccessful attempt to sink a pit to the Barnsley seam. However, the unexpected depth, problems with water incursions into the shafts and the expense occurred deterred the consortium from continuing with the venture.

Concurrently with the failed development at Denaby, another syndicate of promoters headed by Messrs Goatley & Company were looking to secure a coal lease beneath the manor of Kilnhurst, located two miles along the River Don to the west. The Kilnhurst royalty was also owned by John Fullerton of Thrybergh Hall and, together with an area of coal leased from Earl Fitzwilliam of Wentworth Woodhouse, the promotors formed the Thrybergh Coal Company and commenced the sinking of Thrybergh Hall Colliery adjacent to the canal at Kilnhurst in 1858 (this pit later became known as Kilnhurst Colliery). Two shafts were sunk reaching the Barnsley seam in 1860 at a depth of 287 yards. However, the consortium lacked the finance and expertise to fully develop the mine and, although limited coal production continued throughout the early 1860s, the project subsequently passed into the hands of J. and J. Charlesworth Ltd, the Wakefield coal masters, who completed the development of the underground workings. The development of Thrybergh Hall Colliery may have encouraged other coal speculators to take a second look at exploiting the deeper coal reserves beneath the Fullerton family's Denaby estate.

It was clear that any intensive mining of the Barnsley seam in this area would be a high risk venture and require substantial amounts of capital due to the expected depth of the seam. Furthermore, such a development would need to be carried out by a consortium consisting of experienced promotors with the necessary engineering knowledge and expertise to work the coal at such depths, whilst being able to maintain a healthy profit. Following the failing of the earlier syndicate, a new group of coal entrepreneurs headed by John Buckingham Pope sought to take control of the Denaby estate.

John Buckingham Pope was born on 14th February 1807 at Newton Bushel, Devon. How he came to be involved in the coal trade is currently unknown but in the late 1820s he moved to London and on the 17th March 1829 he married Maria

Law in Camberwell. The couple had six children: Richard, Sarah, Martha, Jemima, John Buckingham Junior and Edward. In the 1840s he went into business with his eldest son Richard as coal agents based at Lower Thames Street. At the time, London was the largest city in the world and was dependent upon coal for its industrial, transport and domestic use and for export across the British Empire. Initially, the Popes acted as London sales agents for Cliffe Colliery at Crigglestone near Wakefield and in 1842 they took control of this pit, subsequently developing it and increasing its output. The construction of the railway network through the West Riding of Yorkshire in the 1840s and 1850s enabled faster transport times to the London market and also encouraged the opening of further collieries in the area. In 1850, John Buckingham Pope and Richard Pope joined George Pearson of Pontefract in the development of West Riding Colliery at Altofts near Wakefield and in 1858 Richard Pope became a partner in the nearby New Sharlston Colliery. Reflecting their increasing presence in the West Yorkshire Coalfield, John and Richard Pope moved to Leeds so that they would be closer to hand with the day to day running of the operations. The great success of their developments in the Wakefield area caused the Popes to seek another coal mining venture, this time in the South Yorkshire Coalfield.

On 15th July 1863, a contract was signed between John Fullerton and his son Thomas Gray Fullerton with a new consortium headed by John Buckingham Pope to lease the coal beneath the 1,031 acre Denaby estate for a period of 50 years. This new lease, known as the Fullerton lease, gave the lessors the right to build dwelling houses for their workforce and the right to take coal from the minor seams above the Barnsley seam for their use and also stipulated that coal must be left unworked within a 100 yard radius of the shafts to support the surface workings. The new consortium, known as The Denaby Coal Company, consisted of: John Buckingham Pope; Richard Pope; George Pearson, a railway contractor and partner with the Popes in West Riding Colliery from 1850 and in Darfield Main Colliery from 1856; Edward Baines Junior of Leeds, a partner in New Sharlston Colliery from 1858; and John Moxon Kirk of the Old Lane Dye Works in Halifax.

At the time the lease was signed there was considerable doubt in the mind of all concerned as to the thickness, quality and depth of the Barnsley seam beneath the Denaby estate, as no preliminary boreholes had been drilled. By 1860, the Barnsley seam had been proved at a depth of 287 yards at Kilnhurst, a short distance up the River Don. Towards Barnsley itself up the River Dearne valley, the seam had been proven 5 miles away at Wombwell at a depth of 225 yards at Wombwell Main Colliery and Darfield Main Colliery, the latter having been developed by a consortium of Pontefract businessmen which included George

Pearson, a promotor of the new Denaby venture. The coal beneath the Denaby estate was estimated to lie at a depth of between 300 and 400 yards which was leased for the sum of £200 per acre. However, a clause in the lease stated that if the coal was found at a depth greater than 400 yards, the lessors could opt to pay the reduced royalty of £150 per acre due to the extra costs incurred by mining at this depth. Therefore, due to the easterly dip of the seams, the new Denaby venture was expected to have the deepest shafts and most easterly located shafts in the Yorkshire Coalfield.

In 1809 Colonel John Fullerton acquired the Thrybergh estate, comprising land in the manors of Thrybergh, Kilnhurst and Denaby from Sir John Reresby. Shortly afterwards, he had the old hall at Thrybergh Park demolished in 1813 and replaced with the present building. On his death in 1847, the estate was inherited by his son John Fullerton who married Louisa Skipwith in 1827 and it was John Fullerton who leased the coal beneath the Denaby estate to the colliery company. On John Fullerton's death in 1871 the estate passed to his eldest son Thomas Gray Fullerton, and subsequently to his brother, the Reverend Charles Garth Fullerton. By 1873, the Fullerton's drew £13,000 in coal royalties from their various South Yorkshire estates and this accounted for 75% of their income, proving how lucrative mining royalties could be. In 1888, J. Cole Hamilton of the Ferrybridge Estate Office provided a mineral valuation for their coal brought to the surface at Denaby Main Colliery. As the lease had been negotiated at a relatively low rate it was only expected to produce £35,000 in royalty payments over the succeeding 30 years. However, additional wayleave payments levied on coal belonging to other landowners and drawn up the Denaby shafts would bring in £30,000 during the same time period, making a total of £65,000 or £6,500 per year. In 1890 the estate was inherited by John Skipwith Herbert Fullerton and in 1896, the Fullerton family left Thrybergh Hall in favour of their other home at Noblethorpe Hall, near Barnsley. Thrybergh Hall was rented as a clubhouse to Rotherham Golf Club and a links course was laid out in the surrounding parkland. In 1929 the Fullerton family sold off their remaining 675 acres in the area and Rotherham Golf Club purchased the hall. (Postcard c1910, Edgar Scrivens)

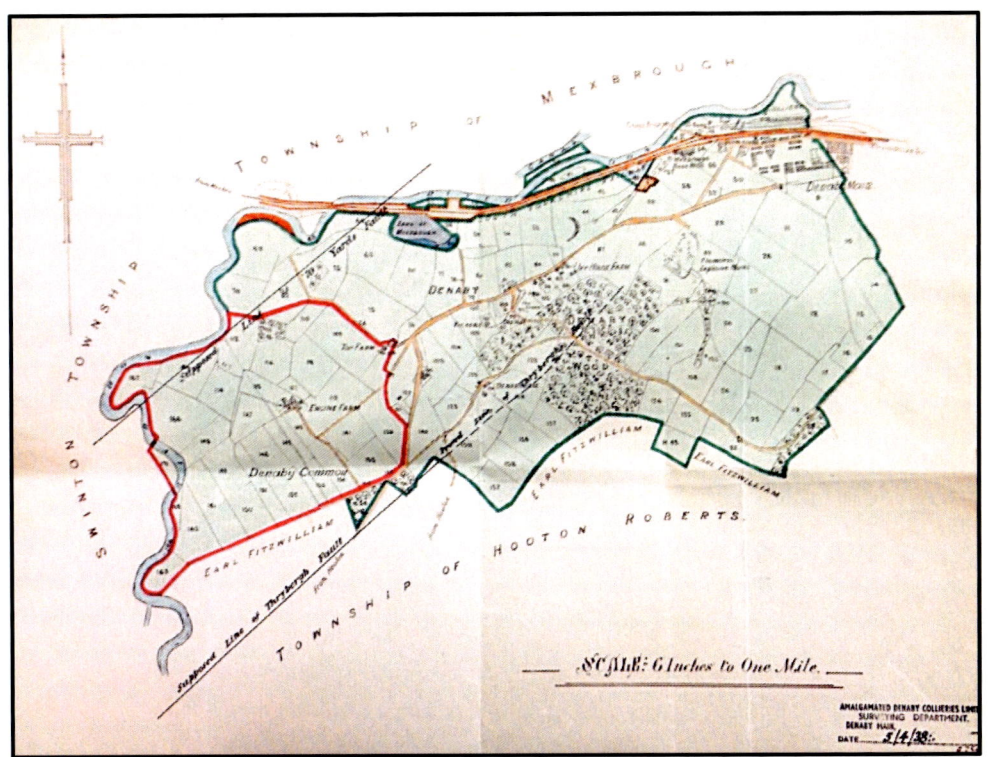

This plan shows the 1,049 acre Denaby estate that was leased by John Fullerton to the colliery company in 1863. Certain terms of the lease were revised on 31st July 1879 and again on 13th October 1896 and again on 17th January 1908 and finally on 20th September 1935. This plan dates from the 1896 lease variation and features some of the first colliery housing top right. Note the Amalgamated Denaby Collieries surveying department stamp bottom right. (Reproduced with the consent of Rotherham Metropolitan Borough Council Archives and Local Studies Service, Reference 63-B/6/68/5).

Rather than position the new pit in the centre of the royalty, any chance of reducing the expensive cost of shaft sinking would be beneficial, and the promotors opted to choose a site at the lowest part of the Denaby estate on a 14 acre field located between the River Don and the South Yorkshire Railway and adjacent to the old turnpike road from Conisbrough to Mexborough. This site also had the advantage of excellent road, rail and water transport links. The South Yorkshire Railway had opened for traffic on 10th November 1849 from Doncaster to Swinton with later westward extensions to Barnsley, Rotherham and Sheffield and eastward extensions to Goole and Keadby, the latter two places ideal for the export market. In 1864, the South Yorkshire Railway and the River Don Navigation Company were absorbed by The Manchester, Sheffield & Lincolnshire Railway which became the Great Central Railway in 1897. Thus the promotors were happy to note that a location on the royalty with the best transport links also coincided with the lowest elevation above sea level.

In 1863, after the ceremony of cutting the first sod, work commenced on sinking two shafts for the newly titled Denaby Main Colliery, the suffix 'Main' being denoted only to those pits that exploited the Barnsley bed or main seam. Connections were established with the adjacent railway allowing the delivery of machinery and materials to the site. A team of specialised shaft sinking staff known as 'sinkers' were employed to undertake the dangerous work of sinking the shafts. The sinkers and their families lived in several rows of wooden huts known as Sparrow Barracks. These were located on the north side of the River Don in the Clayfield area of Mexborough. The two shafts, located 40 yards apart, were designated as the No. 1 downcast shaft, which was 14 feet in diameter, and the No. 2 upcast shaft, which was 13 feet 6" in diameter. It is likely that the work of sinking the shafts was carried out beneath the erection of temporary wooden headgear from which a kibble or hoppit, (a large iron bucket) was suspended. The hoppit was attached to a long rope and hauled up and down the shafts by temporary steam powered winding engines. The hoppit was used for the hauling up of waste material excavated from the base of the shafts, for transporting bricks and iron tubbing to line the shafts, and in the transporting of men from the surface to the base of the shafts.

Almost immediately problems arose with water flowing into the shafts through fissures in the Coal Measures sandstones. In order to overcome this problem the shafts were lined with water tight cast iron tubbing for a depth of 70 yards, which was expensive and time consuming work. Below the depth of 70 yards, the shafts were lined with brick as sinking continued. In 1865, one of the original promotors, Edward Baines Junior died and his share was taken by his father, Edward Baines Senior, Liberal MP for Leeds from 1859 until 1874 and proprietor of the Leeds Mercury Newspaper. By 1867, several minor coal seams had been encountered, but the Barnsley bed had still not been located and Joseph Moxon Kirk sold his share to Joseph Crossley of Halifax, a member of the Crossley family of Dean Clough Mills, famous for the manufacture of carpets.

Finally, in September 1867 after 4 years of sinking operations, the promotors reached the Barnsley seam at a depth of around 450 yards. The coal was of superb quality and the seam was around 10 feet thick, consisting of a lower part 8 ½ feet thick and an upper part 14 inches thick separated by what was known as The Bag Muck, a mudstone which varied from around 6-12 inches in thickness. At a depth of 450 yards, the shafts were the deepest in Yorkshire at the time and as the coal was over 400 yards deep the promotors opted to pay the reduced royalty of £150 per acre which worked out at a royalty of approximately 3 ½ pence per ton.

The Colliery Guardian of 12th October 1867 reported on the finding of the coal:

"The Barnsley seam of coal has just been reached in an entirely new district, at a place called Denaby, about seven miles from Doncaster. The shaft which is the deepest in Yorkshire, is rather more than 422 yards deep, and the coal, which averages nine feet in thickness and is of excellent quality, underlies the Magnesian limestone. In reaching the coal a bed of cannel, rather more than a foot thick, as well as other seams were passed. The work of reaching the Barnsley bed had occupied rather more than four years, as a great deal of water had to be encountered, and more than sixty yards of tubbing had to be placed in the shaft. This involved a very large outlay, and took about twelve months to accomplish. It may be stated that, not a great many years since, persons engaged in mining operations were of the opinion that the coalfields terminated where the line of the Magnesian limestone commenced; but geologists contended that the coal existed under the formation dipping to the east to an extent unexplored. This has been proved to be correct."

The Colliery Guardian report contains a number of interesting findings. Firstly, the depth to the Barnsley seam was misquoted as 422 yards as later sources give a much deeper depth of around 450 yards. Secondly, the eastwards extension of the coalfield beneath the Magnesian limestone escarpment was looking increasingly likely, as proved to be the case when the Denaby promotors decided to develop a second pit at Cadeby Main in 1889. Thirdly, several other coal seams were encountered during the sinking, with the Shafton, New Hill and Melton Field seams showing the greatest commercial potential. Finally, and perhaps most importantly, it indicated the commercial toughness of the new promotors, taking a gamble in an area of the South Yorkshire Coalfield so far to the east of any other active mining operations, and having the patience to persevere for four years with a difficult sinking, absorbing vast amounts of capital without any chance of financial return until the colliery had been well established.

To ensure that the new venture was on a more sound financial footing and to enable the successful development of the colliery and the construction of a colliery village, the promotors registered a new limited liability company on 13th March 1868 known as The Denaby Main Colliery Company Ltd. with a capital of £110,400 divided into 1,840 shares of £60 each. To date, the original 5 promotors had spent £87,600 on the venture which was converted into 1,460 shares in the new concern. The original promotors also subscribed for 212 additional shares taking their shareholding to 1,752 out of 1,840 shares or £105,120 out of the total capital of £110,400, leaving 88 £60 shares available for sale to other speculators. These were sold to George Huntress of Hall Gate Doncaster, Benjamin Musgrave of Park Lodge Halifax, and Edward Palmer of Islington London. The first directors were named as Joseph Crossley, George Pearson and John Buckingham Pope with Richard Pope as Managing Director and Edward Baines Senior as Chairman. The Company appointed Charles Clayton as the first manager on a salary of £150.

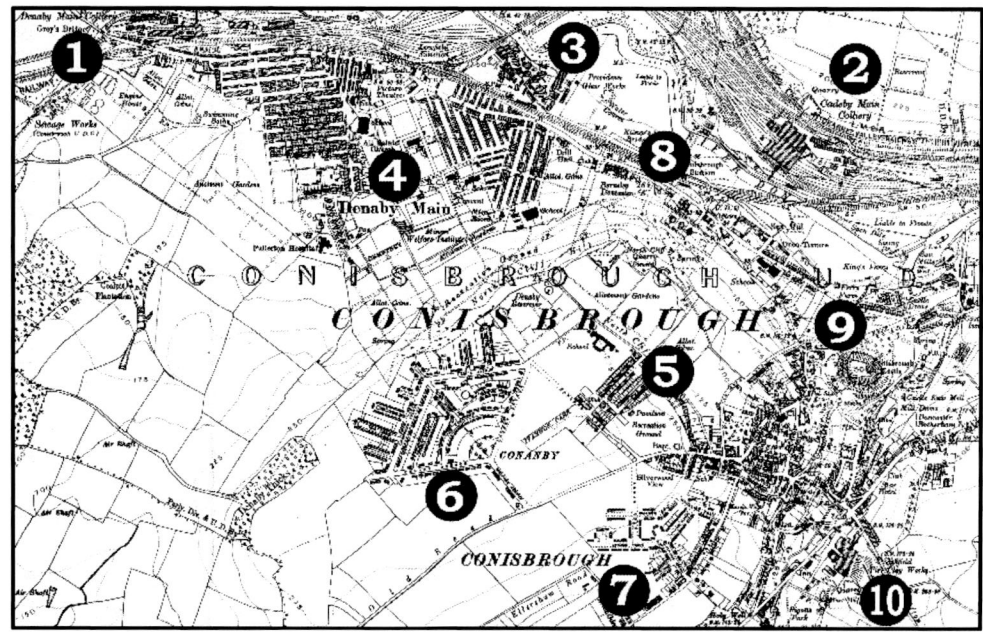

Extract from the 1931 Ordnance Survey 1:1250 map showing some of the locations mentioned in the text: 1 Denaby Main Colliery, 2 Cadeby Main Colliery, 3 Kilner's Glassworks, 4 Denaby Main Village, 5 Speculative Housing constructed 1905-6, 6 Conanby Avenues Estate, 7 Conisbrough Urban District Council Estate, 8 Conisbrough Railway Station, 9 Conisbrough Castle, 10 Conisbrough Brickworks. (Crown Copyright Reserved)

During the sinking process, it is likely that the permanent surface plant would have been erected around and above the temporary headgears, ready to function the moment coal production commenced; the Worsley Mesnes Ironworks of Wigan supplied and installed the permanent winding engines. The No.1 downcast shaft was designated for the raising of coal and contained a cage with three decks, each deck carrying two standard narrow gauge iron wagons known as tubs, therefore 6 tubs could be raised up the shaft with each winding. Due to the weight of the coal and the stresses exerted by the winding engine, the headgear above the No. 1 downcast was constructed from wrought iron and reached 64 yards in height. Arranged at 90 degrees to the No. 1 shaft headgear was the much smaller wooden No. 2 headgear. This shaft was mainly used for man-riding, the cage having two decks, the top carrying 15 men and the lower 10 men. The winding engines were housed in brick built winding engine houses constructed by Messrs Bradley &

Company of Wakefield in 1868, and were serviced by 15 Lancashire steam boilers supplied with water drawn directly from the River Don. Steam and smoke from the winding engines was exhausted via two large brick built chimneys. Ventilation for the pit was provided by a 40 foot fan powered by a steam engine. The fan drew foul air up the upcast shaft after it had circulated amongst the underground workings, being replenished by clean air drawn down the downcast shaft.

With their work complete, it is likely that the sinkers left to undertake the sinking of the shafts at another colliery, possibly Manvers Main to the western side of Mexborough, although their Sparrow Barracks remained at Clayfield well into the 1900s. A workforce was required to operate the pit but as most of the local population was engaged in agriculture, the colliery agent travelled to the depressed coalfields of Staffordshire and successfully recruited an initial labour force of 250 men who commenced work in 1868. One of the perks of the job was the provision of a tied cottage for the miner and his family to live in (rent for which was deducted from the miner's wage to avoid the prospect of any debts being incurred) and many of these families were housed in a row of 86 cottages built by the colliery along Doncaster Road. Additional larger houses were also built along Thrybergh Terrace for the use of officials and deputies. Other workers were provided with accommodation in the Sparrow Barracks in Mexborough whilst the remainder found lodgings in nearby Conisbrough and Mexborough and with the families in the colliery housing.

Surviving records do not indicate when commercial production began at Denaby Main Colliery. Although the seam was reached in September 1867, the first work would have involved the driving of roadways through the shaft pillar (the area of coal left in place to protect the surface buildings from subsidence) in order to open up advancing longwall faces in the south western district. Once established, the advancing longwall face was an efficient method of coal working. Miners would undercut the coal along the width of the coal face, removing coal as it fell, and using wooden pit props to control the fall of the roof behind the face. As work advanced into the coalface, the pit props were removed allowing the overlying rock to naturally collapse into the void created known as the 'gob', whilst maintaining a safe working space along the coalface. Teams of 8 colliers worked along the coal face in 20 yard long 'stalls' allotted to an experienced miner known as a butty man, and the teams loaded the tubs with coal and chalked their stall number onto the tub. This was then conveyed to the pit bottom either by endless rope haulage or by pit ponies. On reaching the surface, the weight of the coal in the tub and the stall number was recorded and every week the colliery company paid the butty man for the coal produced from his stall. This payment was then divided up by the butty man to the members of his team. The butty system was a very unpopular method of working amongst the men, as the division of the payment was often unfair. This was at a time before the establishment of a minimum wage or a standard hourly rate and the men were paid according to the amount of coal they produced.

The men worked a three 8 hour shift system, day shifts starting at 6am, after shifts from 2pm and night shifts from 10 pm. Coal cutting was undertaken on the days and afters shift, men on the night shift being employed on safety work and undertaking preparation for coal cutting by the following shift. The men were allowed a 20 minute snap break during the shift for the consumption of their sandwiches, usually bread and jam or bread and dripping and contained within a metal snap tin with liquid refreshment (usually water or weak tea) contained in large metal containers called Dudleys. Smoking was strictly prohibited on account of the threat of gas, so many men had a tin of snuff or a pouch of chewing tobacco.

On the surface, the tubs of coal travelled down a gravity driven incline to the screens building, a noisy and dusty building containing various tumblers, rotary screens, oscillating screens and conveyor belts all powered by steam engines and which must have presented a very unpleasant working environment in the early days. Pickers (often young boys or men who had been injured underground and who were only fit for surface work) were employed to inspect the coal as it travelled along the belts, breaking up larger pieces and removing any unwanted dirt and stone which was sent to the dirt disposal point for tipping on the adjacent meadows. The empty tubs were transported back to the No. 1 shaft for return to the stalls in the underground workings. The screens building graded the coal into various types which was then washed in the 'Luhrig coal washer', a coal washing plant installed by the German manufacturer called the Luhrig Coal Washing and Mining Company. Small pieces of coal which fell through the bottom of the screens was used on site to fuel the various steam engines and used in an adjacent set of 72 beehive coke ovens, the coke produced sold to Steelworks. Other buildings on site included various engineering workshops, a saw mill and a colliery office located in the pit yard.

Following its grading into various types, (best house coal, second house coal and steam coal), the coal was then conveyed into hoppers which discharged it into a fleet of private owner wagons for distribution via the railway network. The railway companies did not provide their own wagons, therefore the colliery company purchased a fleet of 7-plank private owner wagons. These were initially lettered with the words DENABY MAIN COLLIERY across the uppermost two planks. In later times, the wagons were painted red and emblazoned with the lettering DENABY in large white letters shaded with black which provided a very prominent advert. Additional 9-plank wagons were identified by a grey rather than a red background whilst a number of later steel-sided wagons had the lettering positioned on a black background. With a large fleet of wagons, eventually numbering several thousand, the colliery opened a wagon repair workshop.

The best house coal found a ready market in London thanks to John Buckingham-Pope's coal factoring business in the City, whilst steam coal was used for industrial purposes, typically in steelworks, ironworks, gasworks, power stations etc... As well as helping to fuel the country's industrial revolution, growing in importance was the export market and by 1896 the United Kingdom would become the world's leading exporter of coal; Denaby Coal was exported to Russia, Europe and South America via the Humber ports of Goole and Hull.

Denaby Main Colliery as captured by James Simonton in 1915 for publication as a postcard. The view was taken from the Mexborough side of the River Don and shows several of the ancillary surface buildings, dominated by a large tower, sometimes referred to as the granary. This was later topped with a large water tank. The two chimneys exhausted steam and smoke from the winding engines that raised the cages up the shafts.

The colliery had only been in production for a short time when the workmen withdraw their labour in January 1869 over the Company's refusal to let them join the local trade union, the Yorkshire Miners' Association. The colliery company was intent on working the pit on the free labour principle and they gave notice that all employees would be re-employed as non-union workers. When the men declined they were locked out of the colliery and evicted from the tied cottages on

Doncaster Road and the manager imported a replacement workforce from Staffordshire. Naturally, this caused much ill feeling towards the new 'blackleg' workforce who faced considerable intimidation from the men and barracking and jeering from the wives and children of the original employees. The strike dragged on until September when the colliery company agreed to re-engage union and non-union members alike, possibly due to the lack of production by the newly imported workforce. The colliery had cost over £100,000 to develop and it was imperative to recoup that money as soon as possible by the profitable sale of large quantities of coal and this may have been why the company decided to back down and allow the men to join the union. Work resumed on 16th September 1869 and the majority of the blackleg workforce returned to Staffordshire. This early victory for the men after 6 months of hardship may well have hardened the attitudes of the colliery promotors, whose ruthlessness would be demonstrated in years to come.

1869 also saw the first deaths recorded at the colliery. On the 7th October that year, John Waldren, a boy of only 13 years employed as a Switch Keeper, (one who attends to switches or sidings - passing places on the underground railway network), died after being crushed between coal tubs. Three days later, William Eckersley aged 38 died when part of the roof fell on him whilst he was working at the coal face. On 4th November surface worker John Ainsbrough, aged 19, was crushed to death between coal wagons whilst working in the screens building. During its working life from 1868 to 1968, 203 men and boys would die from accidents at the pit.

During the early 1870s the colliery became steadily more successful as output increased and in 1873 John Warburton was appointed as colliery manager on a salary of £400. However, the coal trade went into decline from the mid-1870s and in 1877, a depression in the coal trade led to another strike when the management decided to impose pay reductions to reflect the poor state of trade. Consequently the men withdrew their labour and the company brought in non-union workers and began to evict the original workforce from the company owned housing, a policy they had employed during the 1869 strike. The management, having been defeated back in 1869, were determined not to be beaten again and sought eviction orders against the original workforce. This led to much bad feeling and hardship and in April 1877, 122 miners were summoned to the courts for rioting during the strike. Eventually, the men were left with no option but to return to work and accept the pay cut imposed by the company.

Despite the downturn in the coal trade at the time, the colliery company were looking at extending their coal royalty and in 1877 they signed a second and third lease with landowners who owned land adjacent to the initial Fullerton lease. The first of these new leases was signed for a period of 35 years from 12 March 1877 and was called the Dawes Lease, representing the coal owned by George Dawes. George Dawes remains a mystery and efforts to establish where his lands were have proved unfruitful, and by 1892 it was reported that the lease was in the hands of his executors. However, he may have been George Dawes, proprietor of the Milton and Elsecar Ironworks and resident at Skiers Spring Lodge near Barnsley. The third lease, signed for a period of 60 years again from 12 March 1877, was called the Montagu lease which represented all the coal owned by Andrew Montagu who lived at Melton Park in the nearby village of High Melton directly overlooking the colliery. The company leased all of Montagu's coal which lay to the south of the River Don, mostly concentrated in the Denaby and Conisbrough areas. On 30 July 1880 a fourth lease, called the Mexborough Lease, was signed for a period of 21 years with John Charles George Saville, the 4th Earl of Mexborough, who resided at Methley Park near Leeds, but who owned land centred on the town of Mexborough.

By the time of the 1881 census the population of Denaby had increased to 1,632 and the colliery company had built 225 tied houses and the pit was producing around 350,000 tons of coal per year. In the mid-1870s, the management of the colliery had been restructured following the retirement of Edward Baines Senior and the death of Richard Pope, two of the original promoters. Edward Baines was replaced on the board with his son Thomas Blackburn Baines. John Buckingham Pope was installed as Chairman and two of his other sons, John Buckingham Pope Junior and Edward Pope, joined the Company, the latter as Managing Director. In 1878, John Buckingham Pope Senior passed away at his estate at Rockland on the Isle of Wight, followed by the death of George Pearson in 1881, another of the original promoters.

In 1882, William Henry Chambers joined the company. Mr Chambers had started his career at Tinsley Park Colliery near Sheffield and had worked at Tibshelf Colliery in Nottinghamshire before being appointed manager of Woolley Colliery near Barnsley. With his arrival at Denaby, Mr Chambers would become a formidable manager and a strong supporter of the local community striking a fine balancing act between the needs of the colliery village and the commercial desire of the board of directors. He lived at Dale House in Conisbrough and later that year, following the death of Edward Pope, he was appointed Managing Director, a position he would hold for over 40 years. With the death of Edward Pope in 1883, his son, Edward Phelps Pope joined the board and took up residence at nearby Loversall Hall. Another new board member was John Charles Cunninghame, the Scottish Coal and Iron master whilst George Wilke was appointed as the company secretary.

High Melton was once known as Melton-on-the-Hill and the village and ancient church occupied a commanding position atop the Magnesian limestone escarpment with a fine westward prospect over the Don and Dearne Valleys. The Hall, originally known as Melton Park, remained in the Fountayne family and their descendants the Wilson family for many years. Andrew Fountayne-Wilson was born in 1815 and took the name Montagu in 1826 following an inheritance. The family were major landowners with extensive landholdings in High Melton, Barnburgh, Conisbrough and Mexborough, and they also owned Barnburgh Hall as well as another estate at Ingmanthorpe Hall near Wetherby. With the rapid industrialisation of the valley below Melton Park and with the shafts and smoking chimneys of Denaby Main Colliery visible from the hall windows, the family found themselves increasingly preferring to live at Ingmanthorpe Hall. Although the Montagu's had profited extensively from coal royalties principally from Cadeby Main, Denaby Main and Barnburgh Collieries, they were also generous in their gifting of land and financial donations towards the construction of several community buildings, notably Montagu Hospital in Mexborough; they also donated several gifts of land in Denaby Main. In 1895, Andrew Montagu died and his nephew Frederick James Osbaldeston Montagu inherited the estate. Frederick Montagu preferred to live at his other residence at Lynford Hall in Norfolk and on 11th June 1927 the South Yorkshire estate of 2,840 acres centred on High Melton was sold to Messrs G. W. Meanley & Sons Ltd, building contractors based at Mexborough, who intended to develop the estate for housing. In the end, Meanley only built 30 houses on Melton Mill Lane and in 1930 they sold Barnburgh Hall to Yorkshire Amalgamated Collieries, who used it as a home for their general manager Captain Hodges. In 1948, High Melton Hall was sold to Doncaster Council and it became a teacher training college and residential blocks were constructed in the grounds. Today the hall now forms part of the campus of Doncaster College. (Postcard by Edgar Scrivens, 1910).

The mining industry had always been subjected to periods of economic boom and depression. The late 1860s and early 1870s were thriving times which had encouraged the development of the colliery at Denaby and the sinking of other pits in the Dearne Valley at Manvers Main (1867), Houghton Main (1871), Cortonwood (1873) and Wath Main (1873). However, towards the end of the 1870s and during the early 1880s the coal trade entered a prolonged era of depression which culminated in a major strike in 1885 at Denaby Main Colliery.

Prior to this, the company had paid the men a flat rate regardless of the quality of the coal. However, on the 18th December 1884, they introduced a new price list paying the men a higher rate for mining larger lumps of coal and a lesser rate for the production of small coal, the latter having a reduced market due to the depressed state of the coal trade. Unfortunately, this effectively meant a reduction of wages and from the end of 1884 the men went on strike and withdrew their labour. By April 1885 when the Union strike pay fund had run out, 1,200 people had been evicted from the Company's tied cottages causing much poverty and hardship, with families living in tents and reliant upon begging missions to the local towns and villages for food donations. The Company hoped to re-open the pit by importing men to work the colliery from Staffordshire like they had during previous disputes and another blackleg workforce was brought in. However, this led to increasing tensions and rioting amongst the original workforce who successfully persuaded the Staffordshire miners to return home. Unfortunately, by now all the Yorkshire coal owners wanted to impose a 10% wage reduction due to the depression within the industry and with no money, no homes and no food and facing starvation, the Denaby workforce agreed to return to work under the new conditions and new price lists, effectively taking a 40% pay cut. However, the colliery management, with their victory over the men, were able to pick and choose who they wished to re-employ and many of the troublemakers and strike leaders were not re-engaged and several had to leave the area to find careers in different industries.

Despite this defeat for the workforce, trade gradually improved throughout the 1880s, and by 1887 the colliery was employing 1,500 men who produced 500,000 tons of coal, believed to be the highest output of any pit in the country. However hardship would return when on Christmas Day 1887, a fire started in No. 2 engine house spreading to the wooden surface buildings and destroying the wooden upcast headgear above No. 2 shaft and ultimately damaging the iron headgear of No. 1 shaft. Fortunately, the pit was not operational due to the Christmas holidays, although 11 men were underground undertaking safety work. As the local fire brigades fought the flames, a rope was attached to a pit locomotive which was used to haul the 11 men up the No. 1 shaft whilst crowds of spectators cheered on. By the end of the day the flames had been brought under control, but the fire had the effect of throwing 1,500 men out of work. This caused the establishment of the Denaby Main Disaster Relief Fund (to which Andrew Montagu of Melton Park donated £20) to assist with the hardship of the men and the families whilst the colliery was reconstructed.

The Worsley Mesnes Ironworks of Wigan supplied a replacement winding engine for No. 1 shaft and installed an iron headgear, replacing the former wooden headgear destroyed in the fire. Apart from the brick built winding engine houses, most of the other surface buildings had been constructed from wood and had also been ruined by the fire, their replacements being steel framed structures clad in flame proof corrugated iron sheeting. The rebuilding of the colliery was undertaken at such a speed that within a few months, the pit had re-engaged all of the original workforce. Incidentally, it would not be for another 24 years before the implementation of the Mines Act (1911) that wooden headgears were prohibited from being used at all new shafts.

Denaby Main Colliery as recorded on a postcard issued by The Doncaster Rotophoto Company in 1920 depicting the colliery headgears, the chimneys and the screen buildings with the Luhrig coal washing plant on the far right. The remains of Samuel Meggitt's Mexborough Bone Mills can be seen in the foreground.

The original Fullerton lease signed in 1863 had seen the colliery company secure a coal royalty of approximately 1,031 acres, which despite the colliery fire in 1877 and several periods of industrial unrest, had been worked very successfully and profitably during the first 25 years of the colliery's life. The royalty had been increased with the addition of the Dawes Lease, the Montagu Lease and the Mexborough Lease, increasing the acreage to approximately 3,000 acres. With extremely favourable trading conditions in the late 1880s the Company decided to seek control of additional coal royalties which could either be worked by their existing pit or exploited by the sinking of new pits, thus securing the Company's future into the 20th Century. Most of the land to the north of the River Don in the Mexborough and High Melton areas was owned by Andrew Montagu of Melton

Park. To the west, Earl Fitzwilliam of Wentworth Woodhouse was the owner of a large estate centred on Hooton Roberts. To the south, Countess Yarbrough of Brocklesby Park in Lincolnshire owned the manor of Conisbrough. However, to the east was the 3,915 acres Sprotborough (now spelt Sprotbrough) estate belonging to Sir Charles & Dame Georgina Watson-Copley of Sprotbrough Hall.

Sir Godfrey Copley constructed Sprotbrough Hall in 1685, replacing an earlier house owned by the family. The estate passed into the hands of various other relations who assumed the Copley name and was owned by Sir Charles and Dame Georgina Watson-Copley in 1888 when the Denaby Main Colliery Company made enquiries about leasing the mineral rights. Charles and Georgina's daughter Selina Frances Watson-Copley married Brigadier General Sir Robert Calverley Allington Bewicke-Copley. Sir Robert and Selina both died in 1923 and their son, Robert Godfrey Bewicke-Copley, the 5th Baron Cromwell, was left with extensive death duties. Consequently he sold the estate in 1925 and the hall was demolished in 1926 and houses were laid out in the park. However, Baron Cromwell retained the mineral rights and during the late 1920s he was embroiled in a legal dispute with Yorkshire Amalgamated Collieries over the sub-leasing of the Barnsley coal seam beneath part of the estate to other colliery companies. (Postcard by Edgar Scrivens, 1910).

The Sprotbrough Hall estate, located mainly on the undeveloped concealed coalfield of Doncaster, therefore presented an attractive coal royalty and one which the Denaby Main Colliery Company chose to exploit as their fifth coal lease. On the 14th June 1888, Dame Georgina Watson-Copley signed a contract known as the Copley Lease, for the right to extract the Barnsley seam beneath her estate for a period of 60 years. The royalty payable of £125 per acre of coal worked amounted to approximately 2.75d per ton. Interestingly this royalty was less than the 3d per ton negotiated some 25 years earlier with John Fullerton of Thrybergh Hall when Denaby Main Colliery was first established, possibly reflecting a 'bulk buy' as the Copley estate was nearly 4 times the size of the Fullerton royalty. The coal lease also included a wayleave of £10 per acre for any coal belonging to adjacent landowners and brought to the surface at pits developed on the Copley estate. The contract also stipulated that after 60 years, any mines and assets would become the property of Dame Georgina Copley. The agreement also allocated two 50 acre plots with surface rights to the colliery company for the establishment of two proposed collieries at the western and eastern extremities of the royalty. Consequently, a 50 acre site at the western end was chosen on the north bank of the River Don near Conisbrough Railway Station and to the south of the village of Cadeby in order to develop a new pit known as Cadeby Main Colliery. A second 50 acre site was allocated at the eastern end of the royalty near the Great North Road, a site for developing another pit called Sprotbrough Main Colliery.

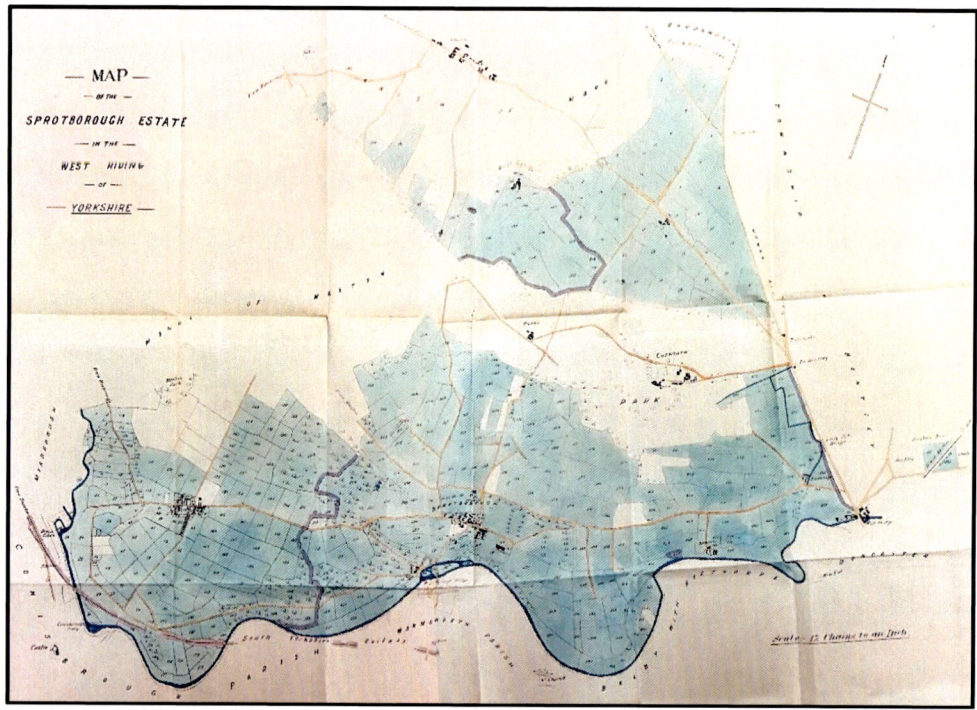

Map of the Sprotbrough estate showing the 3,915 acres of mineral rights (shaded blue) leased to the Denaby Main Colliery Company Ltd. The southern boundary of this large estate stretched from the confluence of the River Don and Dearne adjacent to Denaby Main Colliery, along the northern side of the River Don as far as the Great North Road in Doncaster, some 6 miles to the east. A detached portion of the estate to the north was centred on Scawsby Hall and between the two areas was the Melton Park estate belonging to Andrew Montagu and the Cusworth Hall estate belonging to Lady Isabella Battie-Wrightson. The initial option to lease the coal was granted by Sir Charles Watson-Copley on 14th March 1888, but following his death shortly afterwards, the lease was signed by his wife Dame Georgina Watson-Copley on the 14th June 1888. (Reproduced with the consent of Rotherham Metropolitan Borough Council Archives & Local Studies Service, Reference 63-B/6/14/8).

At Denaby Main Colliery, the Barnsley seam had been discovered at a depth of 450 yards in a block of undisturbed Coal Measures strata bounded by two parallel fractures or geological faults, located approximately 3 miles apart. These faults are known as the Northerly and Southerly Don Faults and extend from the Sheffield area north-eastwards towards Conisbrough and High Melton and form part of the 'Don Monocline' – a prominent geological feature within the South Yorkshire Coalfield. As one travels southwards across each of these faults, the fractures displace the strata downwards on their south-eastern sides to much deeper depths. The fracturing of the strata also caused the inclination of the seams to increase in the vicinity of the faults before levelling out on the other side. The combination of fold and fault therefore resulted in displacing the coal seams by around 300 yards, consequently ensuring that the Barnsley seam would lie at a much greater depth at Cadeby Main Colliery.

However, the mining engineers were aware of this geological structure and faced with the prospects of sinking the deepest and most easterly shafts in Yorkshire, the first sod at the new pit was cut by Edward Phelps Pope on 25th March 1889. The site chosen was located on the meadows to the north of the River Don and the Great Central Railway and beneath the limestone escarpment which guarded the entrance to the Don Gorge. On an embanked site high above the Great Central Railway, two 16 feet diameter shafts were sunk 87 yards apart, the eastern shaft being designated as the No. 1 downcast and the western shaft being the No. 2 upcast shaft. Initially men had to be ferried to the site across the River Don by boat before the opening in June 1892 of a substantial iron girder bridge.

The sinking of Denaby Main Colliery 25 years earlier had been particularly troublesome and the same difficulties were expected at the new Cadeby Main Colliery. A team of specialised sinkers undertook the difficult job of shaft sinking using temporary timber headgear erected above each shaft, connected to temporary steam powered winding engines. The sinkers immediately encountered complications with sinking through unconsolidated boulder clay just below the surface. Beneath this, water began to flood the shafts from the fissured sandstones of the Coal Measures. Such was the volume of water that four pumping engines were deployed in each shaft and the shafts were lined for a depth of 140 yards with water-tight cast iron tubbing in order to hold back the flow. This difficult work would take two years and include the installation of a permanent water pump which would supply a reservoir built high above the pit on Cadeby Cliffs in order to serve the colliery's Lancashire boilers. Near the village of Cadeby, a brickworks was opened to supply the vast quantity of bricks required in the operations.

This photograph from c1893 shows one of the temporary wooden headgears and winding engines above No. 2 upcast shaft; these were used for shaft sinking purposes. The temporary sinking engines were supplied by Bradley & Company of Wakefield. A permanent steel lattice headgear has already been erected above No. 1 downcast shaft. However, the temporary wooden headgear at No. 2 shaft remained in place for several years before it was replaced with a permanent steel structure encased in a brick collar. (Conisbrough & Denaby Main Heritage Group Collection)

On 29th July 1893, the Barnsley seam of coal, with a thickness of nearly 10 feet, was struck at a depth of 739 yards in the No. 2 shaft followed shortly after when the No. 1 shaft reached coal at a depth of 750 yards, the discrepancy accounted for by a minor fault displacing the strata between the shafts. Back in 1867, Denaby Main Colliery had held the record for the deepest shafts in Yorkshire at 450 yards, and although this depth had been exceeded by South Kirkby Colliery in 1878 when the Barnsley seam was found at a depth of 634 yards, Cadeby Main now reclaimed the record for the deepest shafts in the county, as well as being the pit located the furthest east on the Yorkshire Coalfield. Cadeby Main colliery was also the first pit built specifically to exploit coal from beneath the concealed coalfield of Doncaster, whose massive coal reserves would be eventually exploited by numerous other collieries sunk in the period 1905-1925.

Concurrently with sinking the shafts, several of the surface buildings were erected so that coal production could commence the moment the seam was discovered. Steel lattice headgears were built above both shafts which were both equipped for coal winding. Each headgear was attached to a corresponding winding engine house in which steam powered winding engines were installed by John Fowler &

Company of Leeds. Steam and smoke was exhausted via a 180 foot high brick chimney. Between the two shafts, large screen buildings were constructed together with a Luhrig coal washing plant. This proved unreliable and was replaced in 1898 by a coal washing plant supplied by Humboldt Engineering Works - like Luhrig, another German manufacturer. This was eventually supplemented in 1904 with a Baum washery with a capacity of 1250 tons per day supplied by Simon Carves of Manchester. To the east, 180 Beehive coke ovens were constructed to process the small coal which had a very limited market and extensive railway sidings were laid out to connect the pit with the Great Central Railway. Following the leaving of a 300 yard wide pillar of coal to protect the surface buildings from subsidence, advancing longwall coal faces were opened out to be worked under the same methods as at Denaby Main Colliery.

In 1892, the Denaby Main Colliery Company held a capital of £110,400 which had been sufficient to develop the pit with the building of houses and colliery expansion expenses having been paid for by the issue of £60,000 in debentures and the mortgaging of the Company's assets. However, the development of the second pit at Cadeby would require large amounts of capital. On 8th August 1893, the company was restructured as The Denaby and Cadeby Main Collieries Ltd and the capital was increased to £800,000, believed to be sufficient to oversee the development of Cadeby Main and pay for the construction of an extension to the colliery village to house the new workforce, build a new railway line and pay for a foray into the shipping and export industry.

In 1895, Cadeby Main Colliery commenced full production and the first accidental deaths were recorded at the pit that year. On 9th February, E. Robshaw aged 32 was run over by wagons in the sidings, dying from his injuries 3 months later. On 21st February, J. Oldfield aged 15 was run over by tubs underground. On 4 November, A. Hunter aged 20 was involved in a horrific death when, cleaning the winding engine, the engine crank struck his head. During the life of Cadeby Main Colliery from 1895 to 1987 there would be a total of 218 deaths at the pit.

The colliery company had been dissatisfied with the service provided and charges made by the Great Central Railway in transporting their coal to the various ports and markets. Consequently they decided to build their own railway from Denaby to Wrangbrook Junction where it would meet the Hull and Barnsley Railway's main line to Alexandra Dock in Hull. On the 14th August 1890, on receiving parliamentary approval, the South Yorkshire Junction Railway (SYJR) was promoted as a subsidiary railway company with a capital of £180,000 with John Buckingham Pope as Chairman. A partnership was made with the Hull & Barnsley Railway (H&BR) who would operate the line on behalf of the company who guaranteed to export at least 310,000 tons of coal every year for the next 21 years via the line to Hull. Work commenced in 1892 and the single track railway line ran from Denaby Main Colliery yard over a new bridge constructed across the River Don and behind the site of the new Cadeby Main Colliery with a spur to tap the proposed traffic from the new pit, the line opening for business on 1st September 1894. From Cadeby, the single track formation passed through a tunnel and onwards, with railway stations provided at Sprotbrough and Pickburn, to Wrangbrook Junction. Although intended as a mineral line, a limited passenger service was operated from a new station at Lowfield adjacent to Doncaster Road in Denaby Main and calling at Sprotbrough Station before terminating at Pickburn Station with two return trips provided every day. Unsurprisingly, the passenger service was not well used and was withdrawn in 1903. However, the freight traffic was an immediate success and by 1912, over 1,000,000 tons was transported along this line for export via Alexandra Docks in Hull.

A splendid view of the partially enclosed upcast No. 2 headgear and winding engine house at Cadeby Main Colliery, published as a postcard by R. J. Rossor and dating from c1910. In the foreground, rows of 7 plank private owner wagons all bear the name DENABY MAIN COLLIERY, as Cadeby never had its name on any of the wagons. The triple gabled building is a railway shed with one of the company's own locomotives in front of the shed. Behind the engine house can be seen the coal washing plant and screens building. (John Ryan Collection).

With their new railway outlet from Hull catering for the export trade, the Denaby and Cadeby Main Collieries saw the opportunity to expand their interests into shipping. Between 1891 and 1900 the shipping line fleet was supplied with five ocean going steamers named:

1891 SS Denaby (1150 tons)	Sold 1904 to Ellis & McHardy, Aberdeen.
1892 SS Cadeby (1150 tons)	Sold 1901 to A. F. & J. C. Blackwater, Hull
1893 SS Scawsby (2341 tons)	Sold 1903 to A. S. Vagliano, Greece.
1898 SS Reresby (2961 tons)	Sold 1904 to Birkdale Steamship Co, Cardiff
1900 SS Denaby (2987 tons)	Sold 1904 to Glasgow Navigation Company

S. P. Austin & Son of Sunderland supplied the SS Denaby, SS Cadeby & SS Scawsby, Swan Hunter of Newcastle supplied the SS Reresby and W. Gray & Company of Hartlepool supplied the new SS Denaby delivered in 1900 upon which the originally SS Denaby was renamed SS Firsby. By 1904, the 5 vessels had all been sold to other shipping lines for further use. The SS Cadeby passed to A. F. & J. C. Blackwater who traded as Cadeby Steamship Co Ltd. The SS Cadeby was later sunk by German U Boat U41 on 27 May 1915 8 miles South West of Land's End, Cornwall, whilst carrying a cargo of pit props from Portugal to Cardiff. Although this initial venture into shipping had been short lived, the company would return to running their own shipping operations in 1909.

A postcard of the No. 2 winding engine housed inside the No.2 winding engine house. This magnificent piece of machinery was supplied by John Fowler & Company of Leeds and was believed at the time to be the largest winding engine in Yorkshire. (Postcard by R. J. Rossor – Norman Ellis Collection).

With the successful development of Denaby and Cadeby Main Collieries, the company now controlled a coalfield of approximately 6,000 acres stretching for a distance of 9 miles along the valley of the River Don from Swinton Lock to Mill Bridge at Doncaster. However, they wished to increase their royalty even further and on 31st December 1894 the colliery company signed a 54 year long lease with Andrew Montagu of Melton Park. This was the sixth lease signed by the colliery company and was known as the Montagu No 2 lease, and represented all the coal lying to the north of the River Don up to the line of the Northerly Don Fault which would form the northern boundary of the colliery's royalty. This gave the company an additional 2,000 acres in the Mexborough and High Melton areas although Montagu's coal in the Barnburgh area was not leased as it lay to the north of the Northerly Don Fault.

By 1896, staffing levels at Denaby Colliery had reached 1,951 whilst the rapidly expanding Cadeby Colliery employed 1,033 men, a total of 2,984. It was estimated that the company owned 6,000 railway wagons and the sidings at the two pits were said to total 30 miles in length. The miners supplied coal for export, industrial and domestic use; the latter was marketed as *'Dencade- the best house coal'*. The Company controlled two pits, a coalfield of approximately 8,000 acres, a railway line, a fleet of ships and the entire village of Denaby Main. As well as outlets by rail, two staithes were constructed on the River Don for loading barges for transport to inland markets and to Goole for export. In 1897 the capital of the company was increased by £300,000 to £1,100,000 and it was intended that the two collieries would soon be producing 1,600,000 tons of coal per year. With ever increasing worldwide demand for coal, partly fuelled by the Boer War (1898-1902), the expansion of mining operations continued. However, the end of 1903 would see perhaps one of the most infamous industrial conflicts arise in the history of coal mining in Yorkshire when the entire workforce participated in the 'Bag Muck' strike.

The Bag Muck was a thin layer of unwanted mudstone within the Barnsley seam which had to be removed in order to extract the coal. Normally this wasn't a huge problem, but in certain areas the Bag Muck thickened and took considerable time and effort to take out, the removal for which the men requested an extra payment, as it reduced the time available to hew the coal. When the company refused, the men at both pits withdrew their labour from 30th June 1902. Unfortunately, this was against the advice of the Yorkshire Miners Association and without giving the required 14 days' notice. This made the strike illegal, ensuring the men didn't receive any strike pay for the first month of the strike and the colliery company refused to negotiate. Consequently, they decided to sue the men for breach of contract and were successfully awarded damages of £6 per man, refusing to re-engage any of the men unless they signed new contracts. From 26th July 1902, the Yorkshire Miners Association paid strike pay of 9d per man and 1d per child to try and relieve the hardship. Following intimidation of a number of men employed to undertake safety work, the management locked down the pits from 19th August 1902. As the strike continued the company applied for and was granted eviction notices for 750 families who had not paid any rent since the strike began. Increasing tensions led to civil disturbances and Lord Asquith, the Lord Lieutenant of Yorkshire and Member of Parliament for Morley (and future Prime Minister) came personally to read out the Riot Act.

On 7th November 1902, the Chairman John Buckingham Pope wrote a lengthy letter to the workforce. In this he stated that if he was paying 'starvation wages' and that the workforce were 'slaves to the company' then why did so many choose to work for him and not leave? In his letter he reiterated the threat of evictions and urged the men to return to work on the same terms as prior to the strike. This plea went unheard and from 9th January 1903 a contingent of 200 West Riding Constabulary was deployed to evict the families from the company's cottages.

The Yorkshire Miners Association instructed their members neither to help nor hinder the police and consequently around 3,500 people were evicted from their homes with their possessions turfed out onto the street and the houses were boarded up. Evicted miners and their families sought lodgings in neighbouring villages or were accommodated in the Primitive Methodist Chapel, Baptist Chapel school rooms and neighbouring farmers' barns. However, a significant number had nowhere to go and they were housed in large communal tents and smaller bell tents erected by the union and local authority on the fields below Denaby Crags and near Sparrow Barracks in Mexborough. Some families, stricken with poverty and facing extreme hardship, left the area to try and find work elsewhere. Soup kitchens became the norm and on one day the landlord of the Station Hotel at Conisbrough distributed 8,000 loaves of bread.

The evictions attracted extensive media attention and were reported nationally, attracting sightseers to view the tents and marquees. Issue 82 of the magazine, *The Tatler*, published on January 21st 1903, carried the following report:

"The Police were present in strong force and in many cases the goods of the evicted tenants were removed by Constables instead of Bailiffs. Lodgings are exceedingly difficult to obtain in the district owing to overcrowding in the miners houses and to add to the pitiableness of the scene, the rain fell in icy torrents during most of the time the evictions were being carried out and women and little children drenched to the skin could be seen huddled together at the roadside unable to find any shelter."

JAN. 17, 1903   BLACK AND WHITE BUDGET   517

✷   EVICTING A YORKSHIRE VILLAGE   ✷

At the station: Off to find a new home

Passing out a mattress from an evicted house

Police carrying out furniture at Denaby, near Doncaster, where 750 miners have been evicted

[Photo by C. F. Shaw, Batley

A page from the short-lived weekly magazine, 'The Black and White Budget' (January 17th 1903).

The local churches provided what assistance they could, but they were conscious that they owed their living to the goodwill of the colliery company. Reverend Jesse Wilson, the Denaby Methodist Minister was particularly concerned for the wellbeing of the families living in the tents through the cold winter, so much so that two babies born in the tents during the evictions were named Jesse in his honour.

Meanwhile on 22nd January 1903, both pits were reopened for work using contract labour. The Yorkshire Miners Association was sued by the Company for £150,000 in damages for permitting an illegal strike and consequently the Union was forced to withdraw strike pay. On 22nd May 1903, the men, left destitute and starving and in poverty, reluctantly returned to work but found that many of their jobs had been taken by the blackleg contractors and they had to work elsewhere within the pit, but at least they were allowed to return to their company housing, but not necessarily to the same house they had inhabited before the strike.

In 1905, a bitter dispute at Hemsworth Colliery near Pontefract led to extensive evictions of striking families from tied cottages at Kinsley belonging to Fitzwilliam Hemsworth Collieries Ltd, which again attracted national condemnation and outrage and aroused the nation's sympathy. This event led to improved conditions where the threat of mass eviction was no longer used as leverage during industrial disputes.

The defeat had put the colliery company in a very strong position and they had used the power of evictions during disputes in 1869, 1877, 1885 and 1903 as a very effective form of social control over their workforce. Demoralised, starving, in debt to the company and with most of their possessions sold or pawned, the men and their families were ultimately left with no option but to return to work. Fortunately the upturn in trade within the coal industry continued, such that by the end of 1903, Denaby Main Colliery now employed 2,069. With 2,603 employed at Cadeby Main this made a combined total of 4,672 men on the books. However, not all of the original men were re-employed and prominent strike leaders and several union officials had to seek work elsewhere. Perhaps this caused some of them to emigrate, for in 1906, 200 miners left Mexborough Railway Station for a new life in the Dominion Coal Company's collieries in Nova Scotia, Canada, with the terms of their engagement including their passage to Canada and their earnings of $5 (20s10d) per shift for coal hewing and $3 (12s6d для other work).

Denaby and Cadeby Main collieries were served by the Great Central Railway and the South Yorkshire Junction Railway, but a third railway outlet would arrive with the opening of the Dearne Valley Railway (DVR). The DVR would run from

Brierley (with operating powers to Wakefield) to the complex junction of railways south of Doncaster, serving collieries at Grimethorpe, Houghton, Hickleton, Denaby and Cadeby (with additional pits at Goldthorpe, Barnburgh and Edlington opening adjacent to the line at a later date). Passing through the low lying valley of the River Dearne with a branch into Denaby Main Colliery and Cadeby Main Colliery yards, it gained height passing along a terrace cut into the escarpment behind the Cadeby pit and parallel with the South Yorkshire Junction Railway. The formation was then carried across the valley of the River Don atop a magnificent viaduct. Construction of the DVR commenced on 19th June 1902 at the western end and by 1906 the work had reached Cadeby and following the erection of the Don Valley viaduct the line opened for freight traffic on 17th March 1909.

Following the Bag Muck Strike the company spent the rest of the first decade of the 20th Century consolidating their operations. The 72 beehive coke ovens at Denaby had already been abandoned and the 180 beehive coke ovens at Cadeby followed suit in 1900 due to a limited market for coke and more railway sidings were laid on the site of the coke works. The original Fullerton lease had been superseded with a new lease from 1896 which entitled the colliery company to extract two deeper seams of coal, called the Parkgate or Deep seam and the Silkstone seam. In 1909, work commenced on exploiting the deeper reserves at Denaby Main Colliery. The No. 2 upcast shaft was deepened from the Barnsley seam to the Silkstone seam at a depth of 798 yards, passing the Parkgate seam at 707 yards. At the same time a new shaft was sunk from the Barnsley level adjacent to the No. 1 shaft pit bottom to the Parkgate seam – described as a 'pit within a pit' in contemporary accounts. The Silkstone seam was never worked but the Parkgate seam, around five feet in thickness, was extensively worked by new advancing longwall faces. Parkgate coal was drawn up the No. 2 shaft, with Barnsley coal raised by the No. 1 shaft, and the seam was worked from 1912 until 1964 yielding some 13,000,000 tons of coal. Working conditions in the Parkgate seam were extremely hot and unconformable leading to the miners naming the seam as 'the stew pot'.

Meanwhile boundary agreements were drawn up with surrounding collieries in order to avoid any encroaching into adjacent royalties. The Northerly Don Fault formed a natural northern boundary with Manvers Main Collieries, who leased the Montagu estate north of the fault, eventually sinking Barnburgh Colliery. Towards the south-west the royalty was enlarged when Denaby Colliery leased the coal beneath Earl Fitzwilliam's Hooton Roberts estate in 1905, this area being known as the Fitzwilliam lease. A boundary agreement was subsequently drawn up with J. and J. Charlesworth's Kilnhurst Colliery which was also active in this area.

Constructing the Dearne Valley Railway viaduct across the River Don valley commenced in 1906 aided by an overhead cableway suspended between two masts erected at either end of the structure. This enabled the delivery of men and materials to each of the viaduct piers and this delivery contraption can be seen in the upper centre of the postcard. The viaduct was 115 feet high with 7 arches on the Conisbrough side and 14 arches on the Cadeby side with a 130 foot long steel girder bridge spanning the river in the centre. A passenger service was provided from 3rd June 1912 between Wakefield and Edlington with a halt provided on the embankment adjacent to Pastures Road Bridge on the road from High Melton to Mexborough. This railway station, no more than a few sleepers for a platform and an old coach body as a waiting room, was rather grandly known as 'DENABY for Mexborough and Conisbrough'. The passenger service, using a small 'push and pull' Hughes railmotor was withdrawn in 1951 and the section of the line from Goldthorpe to Edlington closed in 1978, whereupon the viaduct stood derelict for many years. However, in 2008 grants were made available for its reopening as a pedestrian footpath and cycleway and it is now possible to walk across this wonderful structure.

To the south, the extensive manor of Conisbrough belonged to Marcia Pelham, the Countess of Yarbrough and 13th Baroness Conyers, resident at Brocklesby Park, Lincolnshire. However, most of this coal had been leased to Dalton Main Collieries Ltd on 2nd October 1901. This company owned the new Silverwood Colliery which was being developed on part of the Thrybergh Hall estate at Dalton near Rotherham and they were looking at expanding eastwards by signing up all the adjacent coal royalties. Consequently, Denaby & Cadeby Main Collieries leased the remaining coal in the Conisbrough area from the Countess of Yarbrough in 1905 forming the Yarbrough No. 1 and No. 2 leases and a boundary line roughly following the present day A630 from Hooton Roberts to Doncaster was signed on 11th April 1906 with Dalton Main Collieries. This boundary line also separated the Cadeby Main workings from the new coalfield being developed at Edlington by

Staveley Coal & Iron Company and a boundary line was drawn up with the latter in 1920.

Other leases were signed with minor landholders. These included the Rev C. F. Townley of Fulbourne Hall, Cambridgeshire, owner of lands in Conisbrough; the Ecclesiastical Commissioners for the coal beneath the glebe land belonging to the parish churches; Lady Isabella Battie-Wrightson of Cusworth Hall for the coal in the Warmsworth, Butterbusk and Levitt Hagg areas; George Kilner of Kilner's Glassworks in Denaby Main; and also George Appleyard of Croft House Conisbrough, Winter Nicholson of Rock House Conisbrough, Messrs Garlands & Wilds, R. H. Sharpe, J. W. Roebuck and the executors of the Waring Brothers, the farming family who had originally formed a partnership to unsuccessfully develop a colliery at Denaby in the 1850s .In addition the company purchased freehold land outright, including more land belonging to Caleb Kilner of Ivanhoe Lodge, Conisbrough and the Lancashire & Yorkshire Railway (which controlled the DVR). By 1911, the coal royalty reached its greatest extent with nearly 10,000 acres under lease and the 4,500 men employed at the two pits produced 1,850,000 tons of coal that year, all won by hand from a series of advancing long wall faces.

Between 1891 and 1904, the Denaby and Cadeby Main Collieries operated their own shipping fleet and in 1909, they decided to resurrect their shipping interests and they purchased the following vessels:

1909 Tug Dencade	Sold 1929 to Torbay and Brixham Coaling Co.
1909 SS Persia (3547 tons)	Sold 1928 and broken up at Preston
1910 SS London City (2367 tons)	Sold 1922 and broken up at Hamburg, Germany
1911 SS Sampan (1730 tons)	Sold 1923 to Abbey Line Ltd, Cardiff
1912 SS Hooton (1892 tons)	Sold 1916 Harris Brothers, Swansea
1912 SS Melton (1854 tons)	Sold 1916 Harris Brothers, Swansea
1912 SS Normanton (3862 tons)	Sold 1916 Rome Steam Shipping Company
1912 SS Fullerton (2811 tons)	Sold 1924 to Culucundis & S Costomeni, Athens
1913 SS Edlington (3864 tons)	Sunk 1918 off Sicily by German U-boat UC54
1913 SS Winterton (3868 tons)	Sold 1924 to Grove Shipping Co. Cardiff
1913 SS Wolverton (3868 tons)	Sold 1915 to Edward Pierre Martin, South Shields
1920 Tug W E Hinde	Sold 1929 to Torbay and Brixham Coaling Co
1921 SS London City (3711 tons)	Sold 1929 to Torbay and Brixham Coaling Co.

Scotts & Sons of Bowling supplied the tug Dencade; the SS Persia was acquired second-hand from Anchor Line Ltd; the SS London City was acquired second-hand from Furness Withy & Co; the SS Sampan was acquired second-hand from Rea Shipping Co Ltd, Sir Raylton Dixon of Middlesbrough supplied the SS Hooton, SS Normanton, SS Fullerton, SS Edlington & SS Wolverton; S. P. Austin & Sons of Sunderland supplied the SS Melton; the tug W E Hinde was acquired second-hand from Arthur Brown of London; and the 1921 SS London City was acquired second-hand from Union-Castle Mail Steamship Co. Of the above, the SS Persia and the two London City vessels were intended to be used as coal hulks based in the English Channel in order to refuel passing steamers with bunker coal. The funnels of the ships were painted black with a central horizontal white stripe adorned with the letters DM or D&C in red. Most of the vessels purchased new had names with local association, (Denaby, Cadeby and Dencade after the two collieries), or leaseholder connections (Fullerton, Reresby) or locations on their coal royalty (Scawsby, Firsby, Hooton, Melton) or nearby villages (Edlington). However, the names Normanton, Winterton and Wolverton appear to have no immediate local connections.

In 1913, Denaby & Cadeby Main Collieries Ltd were given permission by Brixham Urban District Council to anchor two ships, the SS Persia and SS London City, to act as coal hulks in the English Channel. In exchange, the company guaranteed the council an income of at least £800 per year for the following 20 years, raised from berthing dues and tolls levied on vessels calling at the coal hulks. During its first year of operation 722 ships called for bunkering and 677 in the following year. This photograph shows the SS Persia anchored offshore from Brixham with her coal handling gear raised ready to load passing steam ships with coal. The letters on the funnel show a monogram formed from the company's initials D and C. The company also had a number of antiquated wooden schooners moored in Brixham and Torquay Harbours to provide coal storage facilities. (Conisbrough & Denaby Main Heritage Group Collection).

In April 1910, court proceedings were awarded against the company when the SS Persia was evicted out of Portland Harbour, near Weymouth, by the Admiralty due to the decision of the High Court who ruled that the bed of Portland Harbour belonged to the Admiralty and as such the owners of SS Persia had not the right to supply bunker coal to steamers without the sanction of the King's harbour master, or to take up permanent moorings without his permission. Consequently, the company agreed to moor the SS Persia and SS London City at Brixham harbour as coal storage hulks. Their other steamers provided the Brixham Harbour ships with coal and secured a new inland market when they supplied the Brixham Co-operative with 'Dencade' coal for sale in the South West of England. However, in 1911, the company found themselves in the courts again when the Brixham Co-operative Society alleged that the Dencade coal was of inferior quality to that previously supplied. However, the outcome of this case is unknown.

Following the 1912 National Strike, things had just returned to normal when the Cadeby Pit Disaster would shock the region. On Monday 8th July 1912, King George V and Queen Mary were part of a 20 strong entourage undertaking a tour of the northern industrial areas and the royal party were visiting Conisbrough Castle before continuing to spend the night as guests of Earl Fitzwilliam at Wentworth Woodhouse. Many of the houses in Conisbrough and Denaby were decked out with flags and bunting and there was a party-like atmosphere as schools and places of work had been given a day's holiday so that people could visit the royal party at Conisbrough Castle, whilst others lined the streets of Denaby Main, cheering as the royal cavalcade passed along Doncaster Road. Consequently, due to the holiday, a reduced workforce was required that evening to work the night shift at Cadeby Colliery where they were undertaking safety and preparation work in order to get the pit ready for coal mining the following day. That night, in the south district, there were only 35 men working as opposed to the 136 usually expected and in the early hours of Tuesday 9th July 1912 at about 4.30am, a terrible explosion occurred.

Two men, Edward Humphries and Albert Wildman, carried the news of the explosion to the pit bottom. They had discovered the scene of the disaster, encountering an exploded mess of smashed tubs, twisted rails and fallen stone and they had found the body of a man. News of the accident spread quickly and there was a rush to the colliery and rescue parties including the Wath Mines Rescue Station were summoned but there was a fear of the spread of afterdamp, the toxic mixture of gases left following an explosion. Afterdamp, consisting of Carbon Dioxide, Nitrogen, Hydrogen Sulphide and lethal levels of Carbon Monoxide was highly poisonous. A rescue party went down to recover the bodies of the first explosion. The rescue party included Mr William Pickering, H. M. Chief Inspector of Mines and Mines Inspectors Hewitt & Tickle; Mr Douglas Chambers, manager of Denaby Main (and the son of William Chambers the Managing Director who was in Sunderland at the time); Mr Charles Bury, manager of Cadeby Main and Mr Witty the colliery agent. The group were underground when a second explosion occurred killing the majority of people in the rescue team. Consequently, a further rescue party descended the pit and by 5pm that day, 31 bodies had been recovered and brought to the surface.

In the meantime, crowds started to gather at the pithead as the terrible news spread throughout the district. The royal party continued with their tour visiting nearby Silverwood Colliery and Woodlands Model Village at Brodsworth Colliery before taking lunch at Hickleton Hall. On learning of the disaster, the King's secretary forwarded a telegram to the colliery offices:

"The King and Queen are shocked to hear of the terrible disaster at your colliery. The fact that their majesties were near to the scene, in the midst of so much rejoicing when they visited Conisbrough yesterday brings home to them still more the sorrow and sadness which now prevails amongst you. I am desired to express their Majesties heartfelt sympathy with the families of those who have perished and with the sufferers in this grievous calamity."

That afternoon, the King continued with the tour and descended Elsecar Colliery near Barnsley before returning to Wentworth Woodhouse. In the evening the Royal Party decided to make an unscheduled visit to Cadeby Main Colliery. The King and Queen were received by William Chambers at the colliery offices when a reporter recorded the following:

"About 7pm the King and Queen drove up in a motor car. An almost imperceptible murmur went around that the King and Queen had come. The crowd closed around the motor. Two police officers, almost as surprised as the people, pulled smartly to attention, but there was no attempt to keep back the crowd. All was informal, everything completely natural. Little children clustered around and with wondering eyes looked up into the faces of the King and Queen. The King wore an expression of deep concern as though some very personal calamity had occurred. Tears glistened in the eyes of the Queen as she hurried up the steps anxious to learn the fullest details. The Queen emerged with bowed head, tears still filled her eyes and she gazed across the valley to the pithead. A Queen was in tears with a grief that was as real as that of those around. The cheer of the little group, whose loyalty outweighed even their grief, died away into a sob."

After their departure the colliery company issued a statement:

"Their Majesties the King and Queen have visited Cadeby Colliery today to ascertain personally the particulars of the sad calamity which has deprived so many of us of those we love. They have commended me to express to all those who have suffered the loss of any who are dear to them their deepest sympathy with them in their grief".

A series of postcards issued by Regina Press of Doncaster depicting scenes at the Cadeby Disaster. The production of commercial postcards of such disasters may now seem insensitive, but at the time, before the widespread use of the telephone, they were a quick and cheap form of conveying news to friends and relatives throughout the country and postcard publishers often had postcards of events and disasters printed overnight and available to purchase the following day.

Above: *The anxious crowd waiting for news (Norman Ellis Collection)*
Below: *The Rescue Party leaving through a throng of worried onlookers and miner's wives*

The explosion and the attendance of the Royal Party attracted considerable media interest and reports were carried in numerous national and local newspapers. In what might nowadays be considered a little insensitive, postcards of the crowds at the pithead were published for sale the next day and later souvenir table napkins were printed detailing a list of the dead.

By Thursday 11th July, 69 bodies had been recovered. The disaster had created 62 widows and left 132 fatherless children. Many of the bodies were buried on Friday 12th July in a mass grave in Denaby Cemetery and others were buried at Conisbrough Cemetery. At the time there were minimal death benefits and neither the state nor the colliery company made provision for a miner's family in the event of his death. Furthermore, after a short time the colliery company would be looking to take back possession of their company house in order to tenant another worker and his family. Consequently, the dependants of the victims would be reliant upon donations to the disaster relief fund for their subsistence. A relief fund was established with the following trustees: Viscount Halifax of Hickleton Hall, Mr Frederick Montagu of Melton Park, Sir Charles Nicholson MP, Mr Charles Thellusson of Brodsworth Hall, Mr William Warde-Aldham of Frickley Hall and the Earl of Yarbrough of Brocklesby Hall. £9,000 was contributed to the fund including a donation of £1,000 from John Buckingham Pope and £500 from Captain Maurice Pope. Other donations included £500 from Frederick Montagu, and £100 each from Charles Thellusson and the Earl and Countess of Yarbrough. Additional donations were provided by numerous individuals and collections at neighbouring collieries and businesses; for example, a collection from the staff of the Mexborough & Swinton Tramways raised £10 10s, whilst the Mayor of Doncaster's Appeal raised £176. The disaster relief fund awarded each widow a payment of 5 shillings per week and 1 shilling per week for every child under 14.

The inquest into the Cadeby Disaster was held on Tuesday 23rd July at the Denaby Main Hotel. 88 men had lost their lives and there were still 14 bodies left unrecovered in the sealed off south district. The explosion was attributed to a gob fire igniting explosive levels of methane in the atmosphere. At the public inquiry held at Doncaster Guildhall on 5th August 1912, the jury returned a verdict of 'accidental death caused by two gas explosions'. The colliery management were not found to be in breach of the Mines Act (1911) but were criticised for not sealing off the district in which several small scale gob fires had occurred in the weeks leading up to the explosion and in allowing so many people into the mine following the first explosion in order to recover the bodies before the area had been made totally safe. It was not until September that the final bodies were recovered from the pit, two of which were sadly beyond identification, and a third only being recognised by his pit boots. The first explosion had killed 35 men and

53 men died in the second explosion. Following the disaster, three more men would die from the effects of the explosion and Tuesday 9th July would be remembered as the blackest day in the history of Cadeby Main. Giving evidence at the enquiry, Percy Murgatroyd, described the scene when he discovered the victims of the second explosion: *"Never shall I forget the horrible sight that met my eyes when I got to the point where the explosion had taken place. The bodies were shattered most awfully."* In 1913, Edward Medals were awarded at Buckingham Palace to George Fisher, Harry Hulley, J. Chambers, Herbert Williamson, Walter Prince and Sargent Winch for acts of bravery at the Cadeby Disaster. Medals subscribed by officials of the Cadeby Main branch of the Yorkshire Miners Association were also presented to the nursing sisters who attended to the victims.

Following the explosion, the entire workforce had been thrown out of work without pay and consequently they were keen to see the pit re-open as soon as possible. The south district was permanently sealed off and by September 1912, the pit was back in operation; the following year Cadeby Colliery produced a record output of over 900,000 tons. If it hadn't been for the outbreak of war in 1914 the colliery would likely have produced over a 1,000,000 tons.

In 1912, the coal industry was hit by a national strike when the Miners Federation of Great Britain attempted to secure a minimum wage for 1,100,000 men who worked in the British Coal Industry at the time. The strike started on 1st March 1912 and soon spread nationwide. It ended on 6 April after 37 days with the government implementing the 1912 Coal Mines (Minimum Wage) Act. This postcard was issued by Regina Press of Doncaster. (Norman Ellis Collection).

In 1913, the chairman of Denaby & Cadeby Main Collieries, John Buckingham Pope Junior died and his son Maurice Edward Weston Pope, Captain with the 17th Lancers, became chairman, becoming the third generation of Popes to chair the company. Mr William Chambers remained as Managing Director whilst Mr Witty the agent left for Kilnhurst Colliery, being replaced by Mr Coningsby Phillips, formerly of Rossington Colliery.

At the outbreak of the First World War in 1914, mining was a protected occupation and the collieries were taken into government control and the UK coal industry was encouraged to increase production to aid the war effort. However, despite the influence of the government, the operation of and profits created remained with the original colliery owners. Nevertheless over 1,000 men left the two pits to sign up and of all of those who enlisted from the Conisbrough and Denaby Main areas, 341 would lose their lives during the conflict.

During the first two decades of the 20th Century, the increasing demand for coal had led to the rapid development of the concealed coalfield in the Doncaster area, although this had been largely undertaken by other colliery companies, for example Barber Walker & Company, the Hickleton Main Colliery Company, the Staveley Coal & Iron Company, and the Sheepbridge Coal & Iron Company. Denaby & Cadeby Main Collieries had the opportunity to share in this growth with their option to sink a pit at Anchorage Lane in Sprotbrough. However, they decided to concentrate on their central royalty and plans for the proposed Sprotbrough Main Colliery were abandoned. On 26th July 1915, they subleased the Barnsley seam of coal beneath 2,107 acres of the Sprotbrough Hall estate, consisting of the land around Marr Grange, Scawsby Hall and Anchorage Lane to Brodsworth Main Colliery for a sum of £300 per acre, making a profit of £175 per acre on the original terms signed with Dame Georgina Copley in 1888. Similarly on 31st December 1915, an area of coal in the Melton Brand area beneath the Montagu estate was also subleased to Brodsworth Main Colliery for £300 per acre. This had the effect of reducing the overall royalty to 6176 acres of which 880 acres were held freehold. The company intended to concentrate on removing the remaining Barnsley seam and developing the Parkgate seam beneath this reduced royalty once the war was over.

The war years were incredibly profitable for the colliery company (from 1912-1921 the company had maintained an average profit of over £200,000 per year). However repatriation of German coal following the armistice signed at the end of World War One had reduced demand and consequently the coal owners of the UK imposed a pay cut, which caused a national strike in 1921. However, without the support of other industries, the miners were left with no option but to return to work under the new terms.

Towards the end of 1923, Major Maurice Pope and the trustees of John Buckingham Pope and Edward Pope decided to sell their shares in Denaby and Cadeby Main Collieries; Major Pope retired to his estate at Ashwicke Hall in Marshfield, Wiltshire, living there until his death in 1946. In November 1923, the Popes sold their stake in the company to shipping and coal exporters France Fenwick & Company Ltd. France Fenwick owned a fleet of 16 steamers and was formed in 1901 from the merger of William France of Goole with Fenwick & Company of Newcastle. It is possible that the success of the colliery company's shipping operations had attracted the attention of France Fenwick.

As part of the deal a new management team was installed at Denaby & Cadeby Main Collieries with Major George Herbert Peake being appointed as the new chairman. Major Peake lived at Bawtry Hall and had extensive connections with the Yorkshire coal industry, being Chairman and Managing Director of Darton Main Colliery Co Ltd. and the Strafford Collieries Co located near Barnsley and of Airedale Collieries Ltd, owners of Allerton Bywater Colliery, Wheldale Colliery and Fryston Colliery near Castleford. Major John Leslie replaced William Chambers as managing director, the former having performed the role for 41 years, was retained as a consultant and he retired to live at Clayworth Hall near Retford. Mr Harold Harrison was promoted from colliery agent to General Manager, and William de Fable, Sir George Higgins and Hugh Morton Stobart joined the board of directors representing France Fenwick. As part of the deal, the entire share capital of France Fenwick's Washington Coal Company was placed under the control of Denaby and Cadeby Main Collieries. The Washington Coal Company leased 2,029 acres near Gateshead and owned two pits, Washington F and Washington Glebe, each producing 400,000 tons per year.

Back in 1920, the shipping operations had been transferred to a subsidiary company, the Denaby Shipping and Commercial Company Ltd, which had been registered with a capital of £600,000 before being reabsorbed by the parent company in 1923. The Denaby Shipping and Commercial Company was subsequently wound up as France Fenwick's steamers would now export the coal through their operations at Goole Docks. In 1923, Cadeby Colliery employed 2,167 men and Denaby Colliery employed 1,943 men who produced 1,486,244 tons of coal in total, the majority taken from the Barnsley seam. The new management hoped to increase this output to 1,850,000 tons per year by fully exploiting the Parkgate seams within the royalty which contained an estimated 68,000,000 tons of coal reserves. To achieve these expansion plans, the capital of the company was raised to £1,400,000 and £800,000 of debentures were issued to the public. The assets of the company had been valued at a total of £1,846,581 consisting of £1,294,592 for the pits, plant and coal leases, £519,300 for the housing stock, freehold and leasehold land, and £51,429 for Cadeby Brickworks, Gas Works and Water Works.

The full development of the Parkgate seam would require the hiring of an additional 500 men and in 1924 the Company registered a subsidiary, the Conisbrough Housing Association, to seek government loans towards building a new housing estate for this additional workforce. The Parkgate seam had been leased from the Fullerton family on 13th October 1896 at a rate of £30/foot/acre but it wasn't until 1912 that Denaby Colliery had exploited these deeper reserves. On 5th November 1925 they signed a lease to mine the Parkgate seam beneath the estate of F. J. O. Montagu of Melton Park. The Parkgate coal beneath Earl Fitzwilliam's 1,048 acre Hooton Roberts estate had been leased to Kilnhurst Colliery on 15th July 1922. Consequently Denaby sought to sublease this coal, finally signing a contract with Kilnhurst Colliery on 8th July 1938.

The Company also wished to work the Parkgate seam at Cadeby Main Colliery and entered into negotiations in the 1920s with Baron Cromwell who had inherited the Sprotbrough Hall estate. On 16th July 1925, the colliery company signed a lease for 815 acres at a rate of £30/foot/acre for Baron Cromwell's Parkgate coal, 815 acres out of a possible 3,915 being estimated to be the total acreage they could extract before 14th June 1948, when, on expiry of the 60 year superior lease signed back in 1888, Cadeby Main Colliery would pass into the ownership of Baron Cromwell. Despite agreeing to lease his Parkgate Coal, in 1926, Baron Cromwell raised objections in the courts to what he thought was profiteering by the company who had subleased the majority of the Barnsley seam beneath the Sprotbrough Hall estate to Brodsworth Colliery.

The Parkgate seam had been mined at Denaby from 1912 and at Cadeby work to drive two drifts from the Barnsley level to the Parkgate seam had been completed in 1924, finding a seam of coal 4 ½ feet thick. At Denaby, the Parkgate coal had been raised by an electrical winder to the Barnsley level, whereupon it was transferred to No. 1 shaft for winding to the surface, a cumbersome process that had the effect of restricting output in both the Parkgate and Barnsley seams. Consequently, William Chambers and the chief engineer Ralph Williamson had drawn up plans for a new headgear at the No.2 shaft to replace the steel headgear installed in 1888. The new 66 foot high headgear was designed as a free standing structure built from reinforced concrete without the need for the back legs of a traditional headgear.

Two postcards published by Edgar Scrivens approximately 30 years apart showing developments at Denaby.
Above: *The smoke obscured No. 1 downcast headgear dates from 1867, with the smaller No. 2 headgear to the left dating from rebuilding in 1888 following the fire of 1887. In 1931 a new winding engine was installed at No. 1 shaft by Markham & Company of Chesterfield.*
Below: *The No. 2 headgear was replaced with the larger reinforced concrete structure in the 1920s to draw output from the Parkgate seam. This headgear proved to be a difficult demolition job in 1985 when the author spent many hours as a child watching the wrecking ball attempt to reduce the headgear to rubble. (Andrew McGarrigle Collection).*

The new headgear was attached to a new steam powered winding engine installed by Robey & Company of Lincoln and serviced by 9 new Lancashire boilers manufactured by Arnold & Company of Barnsley. The new headgear would be able to wind 6 tubs of coal up the 773 yard deep shaft in 50 seconds and was completed in 1924. As part of this development a coal preparation plant and Baum washery were installed by Simon Carves & Company to handle the expected increase in output.

Cadeby Colliery and its large chimney towered over the adjacent River Don, seen here bridged by the Great Central Railway. Note the group of children with fishing rods, wishful thinking perhaps, as industrial development along the River Don would eventually see the watercourse becoming recorded as the most polluted river in Europe. Today, with the closure of most of the industry along its banks, the river now supports a wide variety of life and salmon ladders have recently been installed alongside several of the weirs. This photograph was taken by Janes Simonton and issued as a postcard in 1920 by The Doncaster Rotophoto Company.

In 1925 a company pension scheme for the workmen was introduced where each man could opt to pay a penny a week (which was matched by the colliery company) into a pension fund to provide a pension for when he retired and 40 men signed up for the scheme. That year, Major George Peake retired from the board, being replaced by his son, Harold Peake, and Major John Leslie took over the role of Chairman. The Company was in a strong position financially and they made an approach to the Chesterfield based Sheepbridge Coal & Iron Company to purchase their £400,000 stake and controlling interest in the Maltby Main Colliery

Company Ltd; this offer was accepted by the Sheepbridge board. This marked the start of a closer alliance between the Denaby board and the South Yorkshire mining operations of Sheepbridge. In 1926, Major Leslie proposed an amalgamation between several colliery concerns in the South Yorkshire Coalfield which would bring the collieries at Denaby, Cadeby, Maltby, Rossington, Dinnington, Silverwood, Roundwood, Rotherham, Aldwarke, Orgreave, Treeton and Thurcroft under the banner of one large company.

Despite the General Strike in 1926, the company proceeded with its amalgamation plans and on 3rd March 1927 a new company was registered as Yorkshire Amalgamated Collieries Ltd, (YAC) with Lord Aberconway as Chairman and Major Leslie as Managing Director with the board being completed by William Jackson, Sir Henry Norman, Sir Charles Ellis, W. H. McConnel, F. J. Dundas, K. R. Pelly and Colonel Stobart. However, the amalgamation would now only involve Denaby, Cadeby, Dinnington, Maltby and Rossington Collieries. The capital of the new combine would be £6,000,000 and the existing subsidiary companies would remain in operation paying their dividends on profits to YAC; shareholders in the subsidiary companies would receive new shares in YAC. The new company would have the benefits of scale and allow the full development of Maltby and Rossington Collieries, eliminate boundary lines between the pits thus releasing 5,000,000 tons of coal, establish a joint coal selling and buying agency, increase coal output and number of staff employed, and pool railway wagons, with the marketing and shipping of the coal to be undertaken by France Fenwick. The head office was moved to 5 Commercial Street, Sheffield with the London export and merchanting business based at 5 Fenchurch Street, London EC3. Telegrams addressed to DENCADE would be delivered to the colliery offices in Sheffield. Following the formation of the new combine, the Denaby management took control of Maltby Main Colliery in order to develop its potential and sold the Washington Coal Company to enable them to concentrate on the new organisation. Total output from the five Yorkshire collieries was expected to be 5,000,000 tons per year.

In 1928, further border negotiations were conducted in the High Melton area between Denaby, Barnburgh and Brodsworth Collieries. In order to smooth out the boundary lines between the pits, various acreages of Barnsley coal were exchanged between the three. This resulted in Barnburgh Colliery working all the coal beneath Melton Woods, Brodsworth Colliery mining the coal beneath Melton Brand, whilst Denaby Colliery was entitled to all the coal around the village of High Melton.

A postcard depicting a scene behind Denaby Main Colliery in the stockyard adjacent to the South Yorkshire Canal. Judging by the presence of a number of smartly dressed men together with other miners, all being filmed by the hand cranked camera in the foreground, the event appears to be of some importance and shows the unveiling of a new conveyor loading a rake of private owner wagons. Following the creation of Yorkshire Amalgamated Collieries, wagons from the subsidiary pits were pooled and examples from Maltby and Rossington Collieries can be seen here. (Andrew McGarrigle Collection).

Throughout the 1920s, staffing levels had been gradually recovering to pre-war levels and by 1930, 3,218 men were employed at Cadeby Main and 2,425 at Denaby Main, a total workforce of 5,643. This was the highest staffing figure that the company would ever achieve and the highest number that Cadeby ever employed although Denaby's highest employment level would be reached the following year when 2,763 men were on the books. However, the early 1930s saw a period of depression in the coal trade as a result of the 1929 Wall Street Crash. Consequently, to avoid the danger of over production and the subsequent collapse in the price of coal, the Government imposed a fixed annual quota on every colliery's output throughout the country. Once this quota or 'standard tonnage' had been reached the pit would have to close for the rest of the year, as any over production was subject to fines and deduction from the following year's quota. Consequently many pits went into reduced working and 4 or even 3 day weeks were introduced to avoid over production and thus exceeding their allocated quota. With a workforce on part time this brought on more hardship for the miners. Denaby and Cadeby had been allocated a standard tonnage of 2,014,368 tons. However, this was relatively generous compared to other collieries, so the Denaby and Cadeby men didn't suffer hardship to the extent that other miners in the country did. Previously the Company had recorded profits of around £200,000 per year but by 1930 this had dropped to £108,585 and in 1931 the profit was only £45,197.

Advertisements similar to these appeared in many of the trade directories of the time and this example featured in the book 'Industrial Rotherham' (1930), issued by the County Borough of Rotherham to promote the commercial potential of the region as a centre for industry.

One of the by-products of a growing output was an increasing amount of waste material being produced from the screens and coal washing plants. Denaby and Cadeby collieries had the advantage that very little spoil was produced in the early years as the coal was mostly hand won and very little unwanted material was sent to the surface. However, increasing amounts of spoil had begun to accumulate. At Denaby this had been tipped in the adjoining meadows in the early days but in the 1920s a large block of land bounded by Pastures Road, the Rivers Don and the River Dearne, was purchased from Frederick Montagu for use as a tipping site. Initially spoil was tipped from a series of side tipping wagons but in 1930, YAC installed an aerial ropeway to enable tipping at greater heights and the tip, known as the Dearne Valley tip, began to grow in elevation and volume. The aerial ropeway was suspended from an iron gantry that headed straight up the side of the growing mountain and along the flat summit where the tipping buckets were automatically upended. A later extension of the aerial ropeway at 90 degrees from the summit saw the Dearne Valley tip grow even larger. This grey mountain of unconsolidated material would come to dominate the view from the bottom of many of the streets in Denaby Main. At Cadeby Colliery, a tipping site was contained within the 50 acres of surface land rights belonging to the Copleys of Sprotbrough Hall. At Cadeby no aerial ropeway was ever installed as the tipping was undertaken by driving rail tracks up a shallow gradient over the meadows by the River Don. As the tip was extended so were the rail tracks and the Cadeby tip soon extended to the confluence of the River Don and Dearne.

The Mining Industry Act (1920) had seen the establishment of the British Miners Welfare Fund whose purpose was to improve the social well-being, recreation and general conditions in the coalfields of the country. The fund gained its income from a levy of a penny on every ton of coal produced. One of the purposes of these schemes was to provide pithead baths but these were initially unpopular with the men, who preferred to bathe at home in a zinc bath in front of the fire. Proposals for pithead baths at Denaby and Cadeby Collieries were put forward in 1930 with the Cadeby men voting in favour and the Denaby men voting against their implementation. Consequently a £35,000 scheme for pithead baths at Cadeby was designed by the welfare fund architect Mr C. Kemp with the men paying 3d/week to use the new facilities. The Cadeby pithead baths consisted of 52 baths and several communal showers on each of two floors. The bricks were supplied from the Conisbrough brickyard and the scheme was set to be opened on Feb 20th 1932 by Mrs Leslie, but due to the indisposition of Major Leslie, the baths were opened by Mrs Stobart, the wife of Colonel Stobart with Mr Hodges the new general manager of the company and the Yorkshire Miners Union leader Herbert Smith in attendance.

Above: *The General Offices were built in 1894 in a Victorian Gothic style. The central gable carried the legend ERECTED ANNO DOMINI 1894 DENABY & CADEBY MAIN COLLIEIRES LTD. They were later renamed as the Denaby No. 1 Outstation by the NCB and were demolished in 1982. (Postcard by R. J. Rossor c1910).*
Below: *The Mining Offices were built in 1906. They contained engineering departments and laboratories. The garage next door housed the company cars; during the 1930s these consisted of American Chrysler models. The Mining Offices became known as the Denaby No. 2 outstation and after sustaining some damage during the 1984/5 Miners Strike and demolished in 1986. (Postcard by James Simonton – Andrew McGarrigle Collection).*

"Don't they look nice, bless 'em" wrote Brody on the back of this postcard to his Sister, depicting miners coming off shift at Cadeby Main Colliery, Note the typical attire of the day, flat caps, waist coats, jackets and scarfs, with some of the men having coal blackened faces and carrying their flame proof safety lamps. Perhaps Brody is amongst the men pictured on the image? The wooden slope on the left was used to winch tubs loaded with pit props up to the level of the shafts from a stockyard by the River Don. Most of the pit props were imported from Scandinavia via the North Sea ports and brought up the River Don to be used in the underground workings at the colliery. (Postcard by Regina Press c1910, Norman Ellis Collection).

By 1933, the workings of Cadeby Colliery had extended beneath Warmsworth and Sprotbrough but the ornate bridge across the canal between the two villages had been badly affected by subsidence. Hence this bridge, had to be replaced by the West Riding County Council, but at the expense of the colliery. Also in 1933, the Cadeby Disaster Relief Fund had run out of funds and a public appeal to raise £3,000 for the remaining beneficiaries was launched.

In 1936, further restructuring of the company occurred with the creation of Amalgamated Denaby Collieries Ltd, (ADC) a new company formed to take over the colliery undertakings at Denaby, Cadeby, Dinnington, Maltby and Rossington as it was believed that they would be able to secure a higher annual tonnage from the government if all the pits were owned by one company. The assets and the £2,400,000 capital of the Denaby and Cadeby Main Collieries Ltd. was placed under a new subsidiary company, the Denaby & Cadeby Main Collieries (1936) Ltd, although both companies would still be ultimately controlled by Yorkshire Amalgamated Collieries. ADC intended to increase their annual standard tonnage by purchasing other colliery companies in the older coalfield around Barnsley, closing them down and adding their tonnage to pre-existing collieries within the group. An offer to purchase The Wharncliffe Silkstone Colliery Co Ltd. and the Monk Bretton Colliery Co Ltd. was declined and instead the company purchased The Darton Main Colliery Co Ltd. and Strafford Silkstone Collieries Ltd, closing them down and transferring their standard tonnage to Maltby Colliery.

In 1939, with the outbreak of the Second World War, the coal business was once again encouraged into maximum production despite the industry losing many men to enlistment. In 1939, 929 men left the five collieries belonging to ADC to join the forces and another 956 departed to work in munitions factories. Prior to the outbreak of war, Denaby and Cadeby employed 4,500 who produced 5,950 tons of coal per day but this had dropped to 3,598 men producing only 2,500 tons per day by the end of the hostilities. To address the national need for coal the government introduced numerous unskilled employees into the coal industry, for example 'Bevin boys' conscripted from those enlisting. Despite the fact that they had been reluctantly drafted into the mines, the Bevin boys made a significant contribution to the nation's war effort.

At Denaby Colliery, poor geological conditions were affecting the Parkgate seam giving rise to some uncertainty over the future of workings in this seam. Because of this, openings were made into the Haigh Moor seam at a depth of 497 yards in order to meet production targets. In 1945, ADC drew up a report into the future of Denaby and Cadeby. It was proposed to draw the combined output at Cadeby No. 2 shaft and close Denaby for all purposes except for ventilation. The introduction of large volume skip winding in the Cadeby shafts, underground locomotive haulage with a fleet of large capacity mine cars running along large roadways and the introduction of improved mechanisation was expected to increase production to 5,500 tons per day. The enlarged roadways would benefit the whole pit from increased ventilation and a modern coal preparation plant would process all the coal at the surface. These redevelopment plans were subsequently implemented by the National Coal Board.

On 1st January 1947 the collieries of the country were nationalised and became part of the National Coal Board (NCB). ADC received £5,721,200 by way of compensation for its colliery interests, although the company wasn't formally wound up until 31st May 1961. Initially under NCB ownership, the management remained the same but working conditions improved. One of the first developments was the construction of the Denaby Main pithead baths under plans drawn up by architect William Woodland and these opened in 1948. Shortly afterwards the baths were connected to the pit by a subway constructed beneath

Doncaster Road and the railway. Interestingly the bricks used to construct the baths were supplied from some distance by brickworks at Swallownest and Kirkheaton.

By 1951, annual production at Cadeby Main Colliery had dropped to 430,000 tons due to declining reserves in the Barnsley and Parkgate seams and other coal seams were developed to replace the falling output. These included the Beamshaw seam at a depth of 632 yards and mined from 1946 to 1966 and the Dunsil seam at a depth of 800 yards and extracted from 1953-1965. Finally openings into the Swallow Wood seam at a depth of 702 yards were made in 1960 and this seam would be worked up until the pit's closure. Mining operations in the Barnsley Seam and Parkgate Seam finally ceased in 1966, the seams having been largely worked out over the royalty.

This postcard published by James Simonton in the 1920s shows Cadeby Colliery with the River Don in the foreground. The large building on the right is the Baum coal washing plant, installed by Simon Carves & Company. A rake of the company's private owner wagons can be seen waiting to enter the screens buildings.

The reconstruction programme originally proposed by ADC in 1945 was implemented by the NCB and by 1956 the whole of Denaby's output was being raised at Cadeby. The original steam powered winding engines were replaced with electrical winding engines in 1958, thus allowing the introduction of skip winding at both of the Cadeby shafts. A huge coal preparation plant was built to the west of the colliery and came to be a prominent landmark in the area. Various conveyor belts fed a large bunker and a coal crushing plant known as the Bradford breaker, and coal washing facilities, screens and railway sidings were laid out. The whole reconstruction scheme had been completed by 1959 at a cost of £4,300,000. This had the effect of lifting production from the Cadeby workings to 650,000 tons. However, by 1964 the coal produced from the Denaby workings had fallen to 311,000 tons due to depleting reserves in the Parkgate and Barnsley seams and the last Parkgate coal was mined at Denaby in 1966.

One of the effects of coal mining is subsidence, especially prominent in the local area where coal seams totalling 20 feet in thickness have been removed from the underlying strata. The first effects had been experienced in the 1920s leading to the replacement of the canal bridge at Sprotbrough and by the 1950s and 1960s the low lying meadows adjacent to the River Don and Dearne were subject to subsidence, the meadows consequently flooding to form permanent bodies of water. Foulsyke Flash and Sprotbrough Flash were formed from coal subsidence from Cadeby Colliery and Denaby Ings was formed due to the effects of subsidence at Denaby Colliery. In the 1960s, extensive river engineering works were carried out in the lower Dearne valley and the river, enclosed by new flood-banks, was routed across a new channel to its confluence with the River Don. Sprotbrough Flash and Denaby Ings subsequently passed into the ownership of The Yorkshire Wildlife Trust reflecting their increasing importance as sanctuaries for birds and wildlife in the area.

With limited reserves left at Denaby Main, the NCB announced that the pit would close from April 1968, with the remaining 956 employees transferring to Cadeby Colliery and other pits in the area, although 100 men chose to accept redundancy. Denaby Main Colliery had been in production for over a 100 years mining the Barnsley seam from 1868 to 1968. Although limited mechanisation had been introduced in the other coal seams it was believed that all of the Barnsley seam output during those 100 years (approximately 60,000,000 tons of it), had been worked by pick and shovel and loaded by hand, without the use of any mechanical coal cutting and loading equipment. Most of the surface buildings were subsequently demolished although the winding engines and headgears were retained as an emergency escape route for Cadeby Main Colliery. The pithead baths were subsequently used as a records repository by the NCB and were demolished in 2013.

Following the closure of Denaby Main, staffing levels at Cadeby Main increased to 2,025; however this figure would decline throughout the 1970s due to the onslaught of mechanisation. By 1983, 1,023 men were employed at the pit producing 327,000 tons of coal but the colliery made a loss of £5,578,000 that year. In 1984 the yearlong national Miners' Strike occurred and the men returned to work a year later. However, by now the NCB were looking to close the pit on the grounds that it hadn't made a profit for the last 20 years. In 1986 the final 503 employees had produced 227,000 tons when the NCB announced that closure would take place from 7th November due to economic pressures. Despite the protestations of the men and the union on the grounds that there were still 17,500,000 tons of reserves left that could extend the life of the pit for 30 years, closure went ahead. The final workforce was offered redundancy or a place at another pit in the region, thus ending 123 years of intensive coal mining operations in the Denaby Main area. The closure brought economic hardship to the district with high unemployment levels, which were partially addressed with the opening of an industrial estate on Denaby Lane in an attempt to attract new industry to the area.

In 1985, South Yorkshire County Council commenced reclamation work on the Dearne Valley tip. The profile of this mountain of spoil was smoothed and the height lowered; the tip was grassed over and converted into fields and woodlands. The Council also begun restoration of the Denaby Colliery site and in 1986 the remaining headgears and engine houses were demolished and the shafts filled. The area was subsequently grassed over with the shafts marked by concrete caps and brass plaques, the plaques later removed by souvenir collectors.

In 1987 the Cadeby Colliery shafts were filled in and the surface buildings were demolished with the huge colliery chimney being blown up on 26th October 1987. Again the surface area was landscaped and the shafts marked with concrete caps and brass plaques. For some time the Cadeby spoil tip remained derelict and in the mid-1990s it was reworked by RJB Mining to extract small coal and the remains of the tip were subsequently re-profiled and landscaped as fields.

In 1987 the Jim MacFarlane memorial sculpture was unveiled adjacent to Conisbrough Library. The bronze sculpture by artist Graham Ibberson depicted a miner trapped by a roof fall with his wife standing helpless alongside him. Later that year a Miners Memorial Chapel was built adjacent to the new All Saints Church in Denaby Main to form a memorial to all the mining communities in the area. The chapel was built from bricks salvaged from Cadeby and neighbouring collieries and the interior contains numerous impressive artworks. Taking pride of place is the altar consisting of a huge one ton piece of coal encased in glass, mined from Manvers Main Colliery, alongside one of the pit wheels from Cadeby Colliery. The Chapel was dedicated on Easter Sunday March 26th 1989 by the Bishop of Sheffield.

In 1986, one of the Denaby pit wheels was mounted adjacent to Doncaster Road to form an artwork known as 'The Price of Coal'. Three plaques were unveiled on the brick plinth: the first one dedicated to the 203 men and boys who lost their lives at the colliery, the second one indicating the date of reclamation work by the South Yorkshire County Council and the third one in memory of Jim MacFarlane, (1930-1985) who started work at the pit at the age of 14 before leaving to undertake a career in politics becoming leader of DMBC in 1983 and a lecturer in industrial studies and director of NUM courses at Sheffield University.

For several years the site of Denaby Colliery lay undeveloped with concrete plugs marking the position of the colliery shafts. However, in 2002, the Dearne Valley Leisure Centre opened on the site replacing the swimming baths at the Miners Welfare Centre in Denaby Main and forming a major new leisure facility for the region. The new leisure centre was designed to partially resemble a pit winding wheel when viewed from above and has become a very successful and well used facility. The increasingly busy A6023 Doncaster Road was improved from 2004 with the opening of the Bambury Bridge flyover replacing the old bottle neck formed by the railway level crossings and the narrow River Don Bridge.

Meanwhile, at the site of Cadeby Colliery, even grander plans were afoot when a local business man, Jonathan Smales, put forward proposals to develop the 400 acre site as a new national visitor attraction called the Earth Centre. In 1996, a £41.6 million grant was awarded by the Government's Millennium Commission, to fund the restoration of the site with the aim that the Earth Centre would form one of the Landmark Millennium Projects commissioned to mark the new millennium and in 2001 the Earth Centre opened to the public. However, it soon became evident that visitor numbers were falling beneath estimated targets and the project was looking increasingly unviable. Consequently, after a short life the Earth Centre closed in 2004. The site passed into the care of Doncaster Metropolitan Borough Council who finally sold it in 2011 to Kingswood Inspiring Learning who developed the buildings and site as Kingswood Dearne Valley, a residential and educational activity centre for school and community groups. Another Millennium Commission project was the establishment of the Trans Pennine Trail, an accessible walking, cycling, horse-riding and wheelchair-friendly long distance national trail from Liverpool on the Irish Sea coast to Hornsea on the North Sea coast. This opened in 2004 and entered the Denaby area alongside the River Dearne, passing behind the two colliery spoil heaps and the site of Cadeby Colliery before continuing along the River Don valley to Doncaster and onwards. The Trans Pennine Trial was augmented with the opening of a spur off the Sustrans National Cycle Network Route 62 in 2008 passing over the spectacular Dearne Valley Railway viaduct across the River Don to Edlington.

Today, nothing remains of Denaby and Cadeby Main Collieries except for the concrete plugs marking the sites of the shafts and the two landscaped colliery spoil heaps. However, the mining heritage of the area remains remembered with the sculpture at Conisbrough Library, the pit wheel at Denaby Colliery and the Miners Memorial Chapel in Denaby Main village. In 2011, the Cadeby Main Colliery Memorial Group was established with the aim of creating a mining memorial to honour those who died in the 1912 Cadeby Main pit disaster and on 8th July 2012, 100 years to the day after the disaster, a parade left the site of Cadeby Colliery and travelled through the village and a service was held at the Miners Memorial Chapel. This was followed by the unveiling of a memorial in Denaby Cemetery to commemorate the 91 men who died in the disaster which was also dedicated to all those that worked at the two collieries. The following day a smaller memorial was unveiled in Conisbrough Cemetery where 28 of the men from the disaster were buried. The Cadeby Main Memorial Group hope to site a pit wheel on Doncaster Road by the entrance to Cadeby Colliery on Kilner's Bridge to commemorate the 218 men who died at Cadeby Pit during its operational life.

Above: Transport photographer Geoff Warnes captured this scene of a Mexborough & Swinton Sunbeam Trolleybus passing Conisbrough Railway Station. The vehicle, registered FWX 919 and numbered 33 in the Mexborough & Swinton fleet is travelling from Conanby to Manvers Main Colliery. In the background, the reconstruction scheme initiated at Cadeby Main Colliery by the NCB in the early 1950s has been concluded, complete with a huge new coal preparation plant off camera to the left. Geoff Warnes travelled throughout South Yorkshire on his bicycle recording scenes of transport and industrial interest on early colour slide film and he frequently regaled the author with his exploits and travels around the county. He sadly passed away on 6th March 2015 and a potential publication featuring his photographic work would act as a fitting tribute to the man.

Below: Two more examples from the lens of Geoff Warnes.

Left: Perfect timing as two trolleybuses pass at Denaby Crossings including fleet number 7, registered FWX 891 travelling to Manvers Main Colliery.
Right: Meanwhile at the Conisbrough High terminus at Welfare Road, Conanby, fleet number 37, registered JWW 375, awaits the departing vehicle so it can enter the turning circle in front of the arched terminal structure known as 'The Clock'.

Denaby Main Colliery Village

"Greetings from Denaby Main" - a Multiview postcard issued by the Doncaster Rotophoto Company in 1920 depicting 5 views of the village: Top left: the pit with a steam train approaching:, Top Right: Denaby Empire Cinema, Bottom Left: Alexander Buildings on Doncaster Road. Bottom Right: Doncaster Road looking towards the Wesleyan Chapel with the wooden shops opposite. Centre: All Saints Church.

Prior to 1863, the area around Conisbrough and Denaby Main was predominantly rural in aspect. The road connecting Sheffield, Rotherham, Conisbrough and Doncaster had been upgraded by a Turnpike Act in 1764 and in 1818 the Brampton Bierlow and Hooton Roberts Turnpike Act (Swinton Branch) improved the road known as Doncaster Road between Conisbrough and Mexborough. An iron bridge was constructed across the River Don and a narrow hump backed bridge built over the South Yorkshire Canal with a toll both located at the junction with Pastures Road, the lane that led to High Melton. In 1849, the Swinton to Doncaster Railway opened and crossed Doncaster Road by way of a skewed level crossing just to the south of the iron bridge over the River Don. The railway employed a man to open and close the level crossing gates and he lived with his family in a small house adjacent to the crossings. The only other building in the area was a large farm on the other side of the level crossing belonging to John Fullerton of Thrybergh Hall.

Consequently when sinking operations for Denaby Main Colliery commenced in this rural area in 1863, it was clear that due to the lack of any nearby accommodation, any new workforce would have to be housed in a purpose built settlement adjacent to the colliery. This was before the time of local authority housing provision and most industrial housing was provided by speculative builders who would then rent the properties to tenants. However, a number of colliery concerns were seeing the benefit in directly building the houses themselves at their own expense, thus providing what were known as 'tied cottages' or 'company housing' to exclusively house their own workforce. This had the added advantage in that they could control who lived in the company housing and deduct rent directly from the men's wages at source. Another benefit was that during times of industrial strife, the threat of eviction was found to be a very effective tool of social control over the workforce.

Between 1868 and 1905, the colliery company constructed around 1,700 houses for their workforce during 7 distinct phases of building which have been identified as follows:

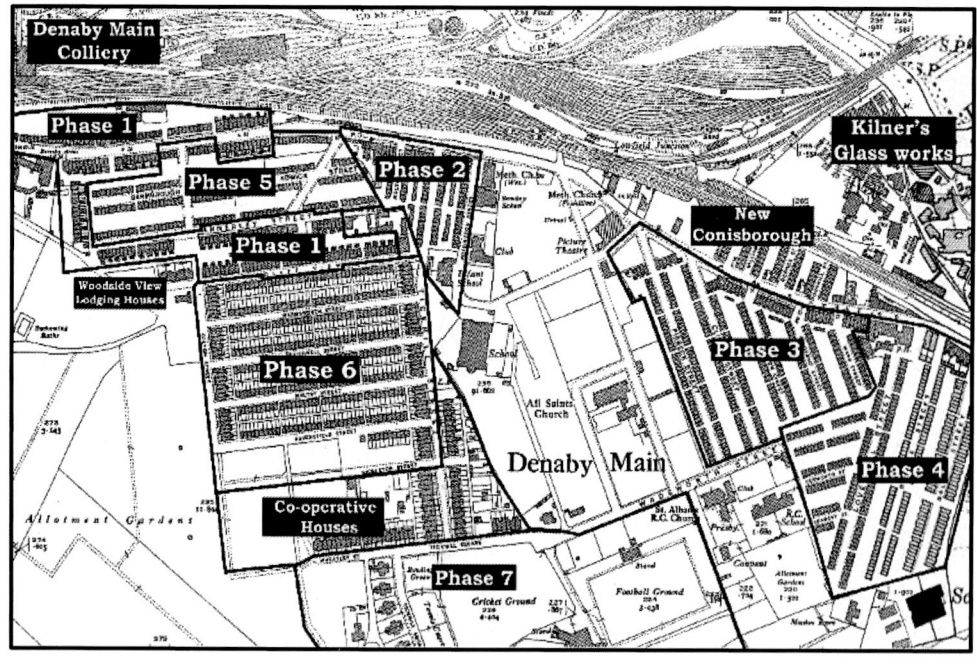

An extract from the 1931 Ordnance Survey 1:1250 map showing the seven phases of house building at Denaby Main. The colliery housing was built in two large groups separated by a central area later occupied by various community buildings. The housing to the west was sometimes known as Denaby Main Low and that to the east as Denaby Main High. The housing provided by Kilner's Glassworks was occasionally referred to as New Conisbrough

Phase 1

The original Fullerton lease had empowered the lessee to build 'dwelling houses' or cottages to accommodate the workforce. In 1868, the colliery company began construction of their own purpose built cottages along the northern side of Doncaster Road. They commissioned the firm of Thomas Saul and Edward Jones, builders and carpenters of Mexborough, who traded as Saul & Jones, with the task of constructing the first phase of houses totalling 225 in number. These were built to designs and plans drawn up by the colliery company at a total cost of approximately £10,000 or about £45 per house. This development would form the streets named Pit Row, Cross Row and New Buildings.

In 1868, Saul & Jones commenced building a long terraced row of 71 houses split into 4 blocks along the northern side of Doncaster Road and to the south of the railway line. A brickworks had recently opened at Conisbrough in 1860 which would supply bricks for the building operations with Welsh roof slates brought in by railway to the pit yard. This initial row of 71 houses was known as Pit Row and consisted of 'two up two down' properties with two bedrooms upstairs and two rooms downstairs, a parlour at the front and a kitchen/dining room at the rear. Facilities in the cottages were extremely basic. The kitchen was equipped with an earthenware sink, a copper water boiler and a combined oven and coal fire known as a Yorkshire Range. There was no water, gas or electricity supplies and illumination was provided by the coal burning fire, candles and paraffin lamps. The front door opened directly onto Doncaster Road and the back door opened onto a large communal yard with the railway beyond. Across the yard toilet facilities were provided by a series of earth closets built in long blocks of 10. These privies, or 'middens' as they were known locally, were built above a trench that ran the full length of the middens and which was used to catch human waste, usually covered with a handful of ashes after each 'visit' to abate the smells and keep the flies away! Every week the colliery company employed Night Soil Men who would have the most unsavoury task of emptying the middens by shovel and carting away the contents.

During 1870 building operations continued to the south of Doncaster Road with the erection of Cross Row, a block of 13 larger three bedroomed houses which had the additional luxury of a downstairs wash house and were considered superior properties and were allocated to deputies and officials at the colliery. Further building of an additional 141 three bedroomed cottages continued throughout 1870, 1871 and 1872 thus completing the first phase of colliery housing. Most of these houses were positioned in a row parallel with, and some distance to the south of Doncaster Road. These houses were initially known as the New Buildings. Thus Doncaster Road, Cross Row and New Buildings surrounded a vacant plot which was used as a large communal yard. A single stand pipe provided water for the houses of Phase 1, one tap for 225 properties.

In 1861 the population of the old village of Denaby numbered 203 (this older settlement did not receive the prefix of 'Old' Denaby until the establishment of the new colliery village in the 1870s which then became known as Denaby Main Colliery Village to distinguish it from the older settlement). There were occasional references to the name of the colliery settlement as New Denaby but Denaby Main soon became the accepted term. There was therefore very little local population available to draw upon to work at the new pit hence the colliery company had to look to recruit families from the older coalfields of the country. By the time of the 1871 census, the population of Denaby had increased to 695 and 97 out of the initial batch of 225 houses had been completed and were occupied. Those 97 houses were numbered 1-97 Denaby Main and accounted for 487 people of whom 155 worked at the colliery. Many of the houses were heavily occupied with father, sons and lodgers all working at the pit. An example is provided by Number 36 where 15 people, all born in Ilkeston, Derbyshire, occupied the two bedroomed house. At the head of the family was coal miner Thomas Shelton and his wife who had 4 daughters and 4 sons (3 of whom were working at the colliery aged 12, 16 and 18). The Shelton's also had 4 lodgers who worked at the pit and a live-in maid. Most of the other houses were similarly overcrowded and it was said that the beds never got cold because as one man got up to go to work, his place in the bed would be taken by another having just completed his shift.

Coal mining was dangerous work but relatively well paid compared to the average wage earnt by an agricultural labourer at the time. Apart from the 155 miners of Denaby Main Village, the 1871 census also records 5 miners living in Old Denaby, 54 in Conisbrough and 257 at Mexborough. If it is assumed that all these men worked at Denaby Main Colliery (as Manvers Main Colliery near Mexborough had not yet entered production) then a total of 471 men were employed at the pit, a very large number for a colliery at that time. Of these men, approximately 25% were born in Yorkshire with the remainder being migrants from the older coalfields of Northumberland, Derbyshire, Nottinghamshire, and Staffordshire as well as from the counties of Shropshire, Gloucestershire, Lancashire and Cheshire together with 14 Irishmen. However, most of the Yorkshire born men were resident in Conisbrough and Mexborough and amongst the miners occupying the 97 houses of Pit Row only 10 had been born in Yorkshire, suggesting that the colliery company had heavily promoted its tied cottages to miners in the older coalfields of the country where many of the pits were facing exhaustion and closure. It would be interesting to establish the methods deployed by the colliery company in recruiting its first workforce and encouraging migration into the area.

The 1871 census also records Arthur Ranson living at the Gatehouse which controlled the railway level crossing gates as well as a number of colliery management living in the pit yard, including Charles Clayton, the first colliery manager, John Pattison the under-manger and George Golighty the engineering manager.

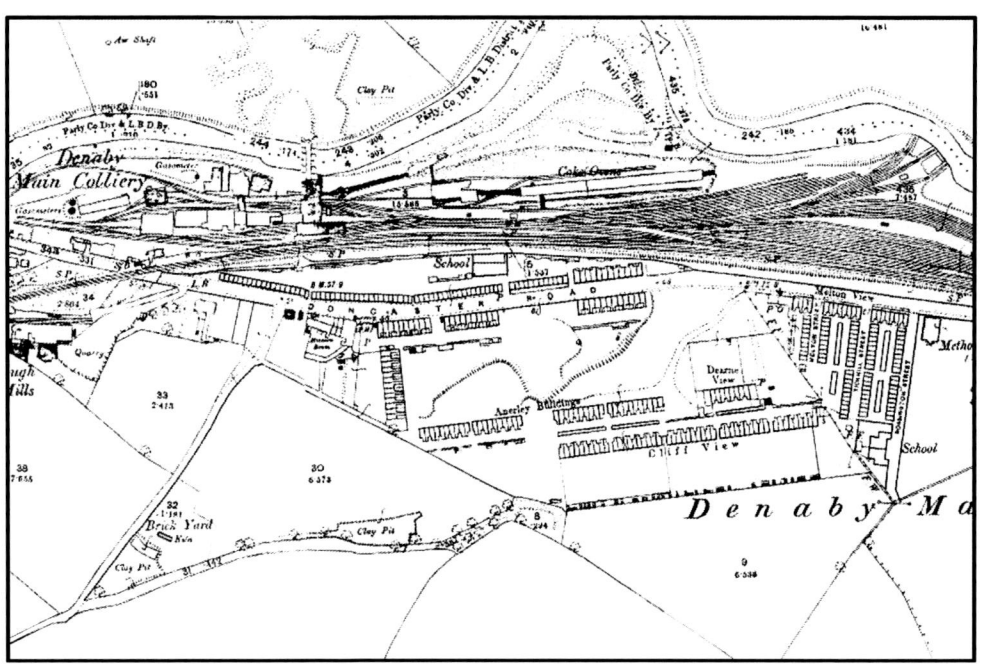

This extract from the 1892 Ordnance Survey 1:2500 Map shows Denaby Main Colliery and its coke ovens with the housing developments comprising Phase 1 and 2 laid out to the south of the railway line. At the time Annerley Street was still known as Anerley Buildings (note the different spelling of Annerley) and the street was completed with a block of houses known as Dearne View. The first village school was situated to the north of the long row of terraced housing known as Pit Row on Doncaster Road. Although most of the bricks used to construct the village were supplied by the brickworks at Conisbrough and Mexborough, the map shows a small Brick yard and kiln with a clay pit nearby. This clay pit later became the site of the Open Air Baths. To the north of the River Don, colliery waste was tipped onto the meadows (adjacent to another small clay pit). This tipping area would later become the colliery stockyard which was served by a narrow gauge railway. To the top right can be seen three short railway lines leading to loading staithes on the River Don.

The Denaby Main Colliery Company Ltd. had been registered in 1868 with a capital of £110,400, the majority of which was held by John Buckingham Pope, Richard Pope, George Pearson, Edward Baines and Joseph Crossley and this sum had been sufficient to develop the colliery and construct the first phase of housing. It was usually the norm for a limited liability company to fund its expansion plans by increasing its capital with the issuing of shares to the public. However, this had the negative aspect of introducing additional shareholders who would require dividends from the annual profits and could dilute the influence and control of the original five directors. Therefore, in order for the original promotors to retain control of the company, they decided to leave the capital at £110,400 for the next 25 years, and raise finance by mortgaging their existing assets thus providing revenue for further expansion and the building of additional housing. Thus on 26th March 1877, they mortgaged part of their operations to Andrew Montagu of Melton Park raising £30,000 to pay for the next phase of house building.

The housing depicted here forms part of Pit Row on Doncaster Road, originally built in 1868 as the first phase of house building for Denaby Main Colliery. This picture was taken some time in the mid-1950s (note the appearance of television aerials on some of the chimneys - many British households obtained their first television set at this time to watch the Coronation of Queen Elizabeth II in 1953). A Mexborough & Swinton Sunbeam trolleybus 36 (registered FWX 920) travelling en route from Conisbrough Brooke Square to Rotherham, has just passed a parked delivery lorry (registered OWT 617) belonging to Peters (Conisbrough) Ltd, a wholesale fruit and potato merchant, who may be delivering to one of the shops on the south side of Doncaster Road. In the late 1960s, Conisbrough Urban District Council commenced the demolition of Pit Row and the area was subsequently landscaped and planted with trees. (Photograph by Peter Mitchell, reproduced courtesy of S. J. Butler.)

The 1881 Census for Denaby showed a population of 1,659 of whom 164 lived in Old Denaby and 1,495 in Denaby Main. By 1881, Pit Row numbered 114 houses accommodating 715 people, Cross Row consisted of 13 larger 3 bedroomed houses accommodating 69 people whilst the New Buildings, consisting of 99 three bedroom properties, housing 662 people. The remainder lived in the Reresby Arms Hotel, Reresby Cottage Mission Church, Reresby Cottage, Bone Mill Cottages, the Railway Gate House and Denaby Pit yard offices with a colliery manager, named as John Slack, living on Pit Row and there were several people living in the first colliery school behind the houses of Pit Row. Around this time, Pit Row became addressed as Doncaster Road, Cross Row was renamed Thrybergh Terrace in honour of John Fullerton of Thrybergh Hall and the 99 houses forming the two parallel rows of New Buildings, were renamed Cliff View and Anerley Buildings. Cliff View is derived from the fact that these houses faced Denaby Cliff or Denaby Crags, but the derivation of Anerley is unknown and this road was later renamed Annerley Street. In 1878, the 225 houses of Phase 1 were provided with a gas supply for lighting from the colliery gas works.

Phase 2

In the early 1880s, a second housing phase was undertaken, when on 1st November 1880, the colliery company leased six acres of land from Andrew Montagu for a period of 99 years. This site was in Underhill field to the east of the earlier phase of housebuilding, but located over the parish boundary in Conisbrough Parish. On this plot the colliery company again commissioned Saul & Jones to construct 101 houses and Melton Street, Tickhill Street and Rossington Street were laid out consisting of 81 two bedroomed houses. The houses fronting Doncaster Road were named Melton View and consisted of 20 larger three bedroom properties. The Melton connection reflects the original landowner Andrew Montagu of Melton Park, whilst the other streets were named after villages in the Doncaster area, a tradition that would continue with the later building operations. Again facilities were somewhat primitive and the houses were provided with middens built between the blocks in 'the backs', the name given to the communal yards that separated the individual housing blocks. As part of this development a new colliery school was constructed in 1883 to relieve the pressure on the Doncaster Road School. This took the number of colliery owned houses up to 326 although by now 1,100 men were working at the pit, therefore a significant percentage were still living in the adjoining Mexborough and Conisbrough areas. To raise funds for future expansion, the houses of this second building phase were mortgaged to Claude Leatham of Wentbridge near Pontefract for £7,100 on 6th May 1896.

Phase 3

The sinking of Cadeby Main Colliery had resulted in the need for additional housing and on 19th December 1889 and 14th June 1890 the colliery company signed two 99 year leases from Andrew Montagu for two plots of land again in Underhill Field. These building plots were in Conisbrough parish a short distance to the east of the housing built in the 1880s but separated from the latter by a block of undeveloped land. On this new plot they laid out 348 houses in 5 parallel rows during the period 1890-1891 and developed Firbeck Street, Clifton Street, Cadeby

Street, Sprotbrough Street, and Marr Street. Once more the names of the streets were taken from Doncaster area villages with Cadeby, Sprotbrough and Marr being locations on the Copley royalty that the colliery company had leased to develop Cadeby Main Colliery. However, for reasons that remain unknown, Cadeby Street was renamed Edlington Street. These parallel rows of regimented 36 feet wide streets consisted of two up two down properties with middens provided in the backs. Larger three bedroom properties were built fronting Wood View and Doncaster Road. These gained the name Strafforth Terrace taken from Strafforth Sands, an ancient medieval ford across the River Don between Denaby and Mexborough. Saul & Jones, the Mexborough builders, had gone bankrupt in 1881 and it is not known who built the houses of this development. The building of the 348 houses in Phase 3 brought up the total number of houses owned at this stage to 674.

This postcard by James Simonton shows housing built during Phase 3 in Marr Street decorated for the Silver Jubilee festivities in 1935 for King George V who had visited Denaby Main in 1912 when he toured Conisbrough Castle and visited the scene of the Cadeby Pit Disaster. On 13th May 1938, Queen Mary returned to Denaby when her motorcade passed along Doncaster Road en route to Sandbeck Hall, much to the delight of the cheering onlookers. She later wrote to the secretary of the Cadeby Colliery Disaster Fund enquiring about the dependents and enclosing a cheque for £50. Marr Street, named after Marr Grange on the Copley estate, was laid out as part of 348 houses constructed during the third building phase in 1890-1891 to house incoming miners for Cadeby Main Colliery. 162 of these houses were mortgaged by the colliery company on 14 June 1890 to Charles Harvey of Ardsley near Barnsley raising £8,000 with the remainder mortgaged on 4 Feb 1892 to Charles Otley of Bolton-on-Dearne for £13,000. (Conisbrough & Denaby Main Heritage Society Collection).

Phase 4

The early development of Cadeby Main Colliery had been so successful that more housing was required and on 7th November 1893 the company leased another plot of land in Underhill Field, this time from Godfrey Walker of Scarborough who owned nearby Conisbrough Priory. On this site plans were laid out for building 307 four roomed houses and 96 six roomed houses (a total of 403 properties) together with the Denaby Main Hotel with an area fronting Doncaster Road left for shops provided by private enterprise. Consequently in 1894 and 1895 Scawsby Street, Cusworth Street, Wadworth Street, Loversall Street, Blythe Street and Balby Street were built in regular rows with communal yards and middens. The larger three bedroomed properties were arranged along Balby Street. The colliery company provided a stand pipe behind the Denaby Main Hotel to provide water supplies for the Phase 3 & 4 houses. During building operations it was decided that a larger site would be allocated for the shops and an extension to the Denaby Main Hotel resulting in a reduced build of 383 houses out of the original plans for 403. Nevertheless, this brought up the total number of houses owned by the colliery company to 1057.

The rapid growth of housing developments during the 1890s saw a huge influx of population into the district, including many Irish families, such that Denaby often bore the nickname 'Little Ireland' in later years. Further families moved to the area, particularly from the older coalfields of the country, all contributing to the growth of the community.

Phase 5

By 1896 Cadeby Main Colliery was employing 1,033 men and undergoing rapid expansion whilst Denaby Main Colliery was now employing 1,951 men and it was clear that further housing was needed to accommodate the expansion at both pits.

This time the colliery company decided to infill the block of land bounded by Annerley Street, Thrybergh Terrace and Doncaster Road and which had been left undeveloped during the first phase of house building in 1868. On this site, which was conveyed to the company in 22nd March 1898 from John Skipwith Herbert Fullerton of Thrybergh Hall, 229 two bedroomed houses were built on the southern side of Doncaster Road and the northern side of Annerley Street, with Barmborough Street (and its eastwards continuation as Adwick Street) built between them. Annerley Street was connected to Doncaster Road by Bolton Street and Kilnhurst Street and Barmborough Street was named after the old spelling of the nearby village of Barnburgh.

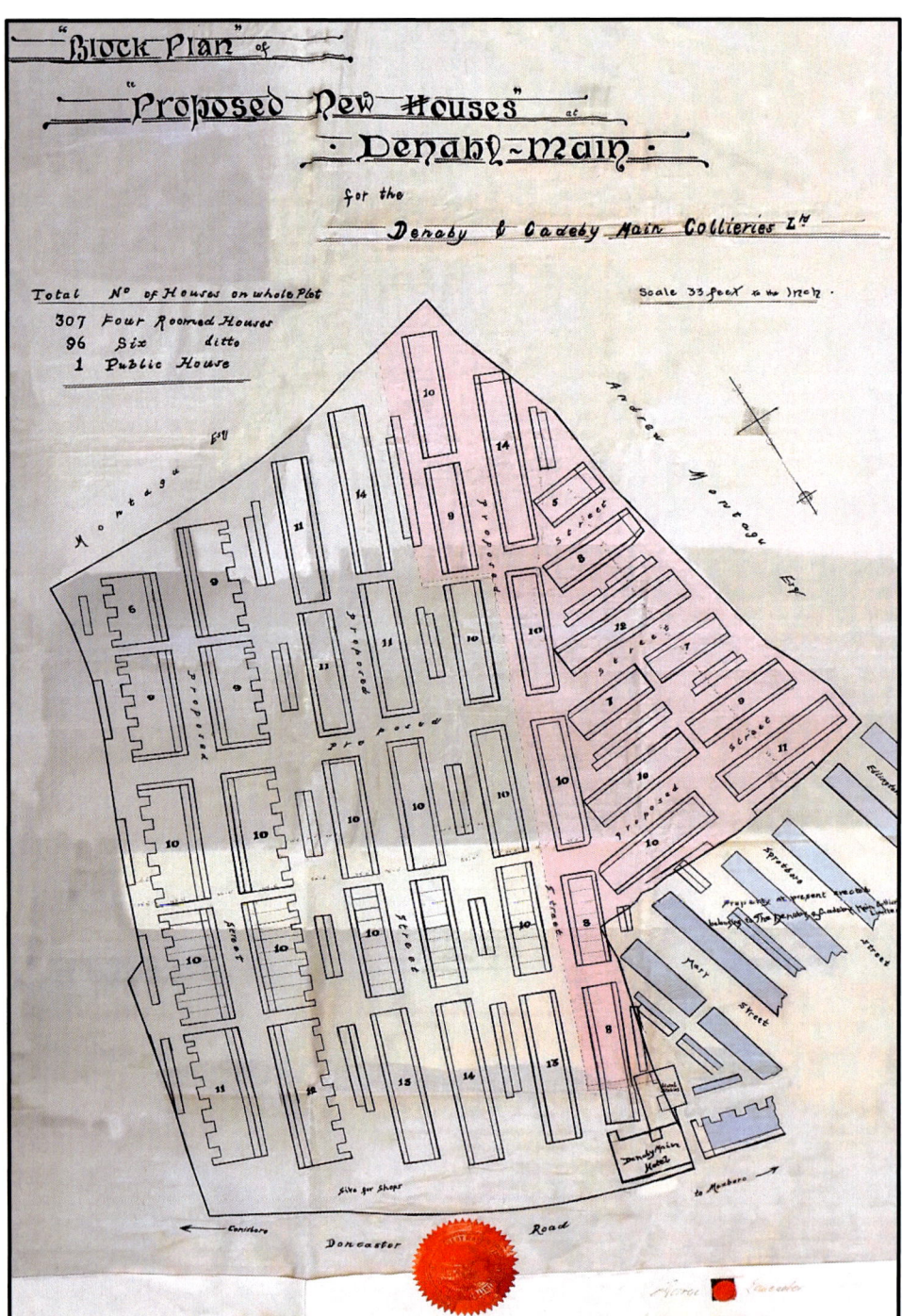

Opposite: This block plan, shows plans for 403 houses and the Denaby Main Hotel proposed for construction on the plot of land belonging to Godfrey Walker and which formed Phase 4 of the building operations. The houses shown shaded blue belong to the recently completed Phase 3 project, and the houses shaded pink indicate the 148 houses that were mortgaged on 15th November 1895 to Charles Harvey of Ardsley near Barnsley raising £9,000. Note the red wax company seal bearing the name of the colliery company in a circle surrounding a simplified picture of Cadeby Main Colliery. (Reproduced with the consent of Doncaster Metropolitan Borough Council Archives & Local Studies Department, Reference DD/MF/1/12).

In 1900, at the western end of Annerley Street a large block of 4 houses was constructed on Woodside View. This building was known as the lodging houses and was intended for the use of single miners and it had 24 individual bedrooms. In 1935 it was subdivided into 8 individual houses. With this latest development the colliery company now owned 1,290 houses. On 1st March 1900, the entire Phase 1 and Phase 5 developments (except the lodging house on Woodside View) were mortgaged to William Dundas, George Dalziel and Archibald Pitman, all of Edinburgh, to raise £35,000.

In the 1890s, water supplies for the entire village were provided by two stand pipes, one in Cliff View and one in Loversall Street. Consequently a committee of miners' wives consisting of Mrs Ball, Mrs Cartwright, Mrs Frogatt and Mrs Shephard went to complain to Mr Chambers, with the result that the colliery company built a reservoir on North Cliff Crags high above the village. The reservoir was supplied with water drawn from the borehole adjacent to Cadeby Main Colliery and additional stand pipes were placed in the village. However, for a small additional weekly rental charge of a penny per week, individual houses could be provided with the luxury of water laid onto the premises. By 1902 all the houses had been linked to mains water and were provided with a tap in the kitchen.

Phase 6

A large block of land to the south of Cliff View was conveyed to the company on 6 December 1899 from John Skipwith Herbert Fullerton of Thrybergh Hall for further building operations; Bolton Street and Tickhill Street were extended southwards and tripled in length with the southern extensions connected by Wheatley Street and Tickhill Square. On 16th November 1901, plans were approved for the construction of 552 houses on this new site. These comprised 400 two bedroomed houses in identical blocks of 10 forming the southern side of Cliff View, Warmsworth Street, Braithwell Street, Maltby Street, Ravenfield Street and the northern side of Hickleton Street. 120 three bedroomed houses in identical blocks of 8 were laid out to face Tickhill Street and proposed for both sides of Bolton Street. Finally, 32 two bedroomed houses in blocks of 4 were proposed for the area to the west of Bolton Street and building operations commenced in 1902. Of this development of 552 houses, only 437 were constructed giving a grand total of 1,727 houses now owned by the company.

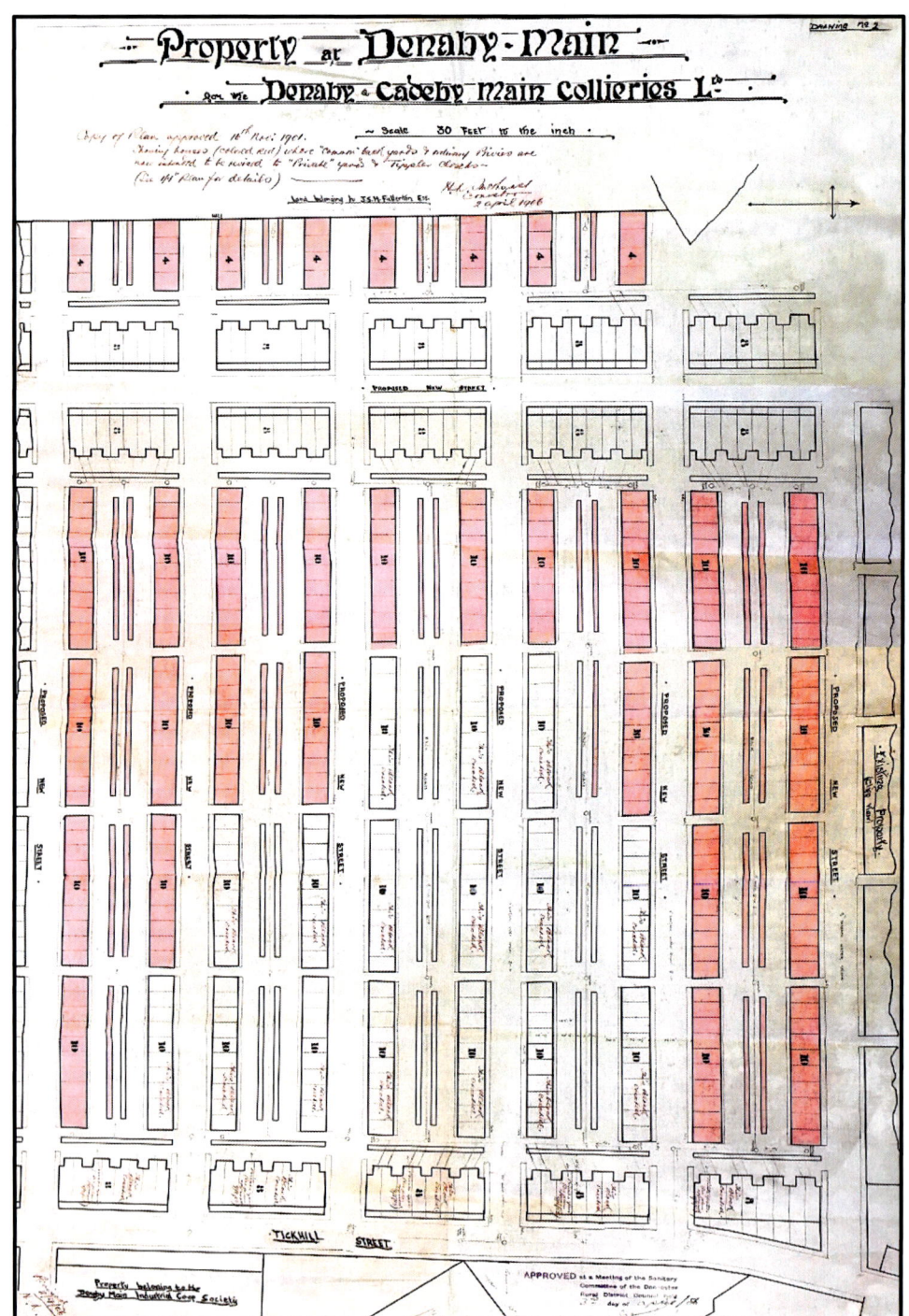

Opposite: *This block plan was drawn up in 1901 and shows 552 properties forming the housing constructed during Phase 6. This development, arranged in an uninspiring grid iron plan, was intended to have communal back yards with the traditional rows of privies as depicted on the plan, but as building operations commenced, the plans were revised by Harry Smethurst, the colliery architect, to provide enclosed back yards with an outside coal house and lavatory provided with a tippler closet, a relative luxury compared with the middens used elsewhere in the village. The plan shows all the blocks of houses shaded red which would now have the revised toilet facilities, the unshaded blocks already having been approved by Doncaster Rural District Council. (Reproduced with the consent of Doncaster Metropolitan Borough Council Archives & Local Studies Department, Reference RD/DON/187/956).*

Phase 7

The building operations were completed with the provision of 27 larger properties for colliery officials and management. A large block of land to the south of Wheatley Street had been purchased by the colliery company from the trustees of John Skipwith Herbert Fullerton of Thrybergh Hall to provide a site for additional housing and recreational and community needs centred on Tickhill Square. On 31st May 1902 an application was approved to construct 16 villas in 8 pairs. These were large houses intended for colliery overmen and were provided with flushing toilets, bathrooms and front and rear gardens with Stainton Street forming a rear access to these properties. At the top of Tickhill Square a detached villa called Red House was provided for Charles Bury, the Denaby Colliery Manager. Stainton Street also provided access to the new Fullerton Hospital and contained a large semi-detached house built for the Denaby and Cadeby under-managers. Behind the new colliery offices near Conisbrough Railway Station, six luxurious residences were constructed along Buckingham Road for managerial staff. This time the street name was taken from John Buckingham Pope rather than a local village. Finally near the River Don a pair of villas named Cadeby Villas were provided for Cadeby Colliery managerial staff.

The completion of the 27 houses for management and officials brought the grand total of colliery owned houses to 1,754 which, with the addition of the 66 houses completed by the Co-operative Society (see later), made 1,811 houses, most of which had been built at the high density of 49 per acre. By 1904, with the latest housing projects having been largely finished, Denaby and Cadeby Main Collieries employed 4,672 men, (2,603 at Cadeby and 2,069 at Denaby), who produced 1,338,188 tons of coal that year. Since the opening of the colliery gas works in 1878, all the housing was supplied with gas for lighting. Finally by 1902, every house in the village had been provided with a cold water tap fed from the North Cliff Reservoir. The roads and back yards were maintained by the colliery company and were constructed from furnace slag and ash which often became a quagmire in winter and a dust bowl in summer. The pavements were built from a hard wearing brick tile with a distinctive diamond pattern. In 1921, Conisbrough Urban District Council was formed from part of Doncaster Rural District, and the granting of urban powers enabled the new local authority to have an increasing influence upon the village. The new council moved into offices next to the colliery company's general offices near Conisbrough Railway Station.

Although the colliery company had built over 1,750 houses for their workforce, speculative builders had built terraced housing elsewhere and while these properties were available to rent by anyone, the majority were taken by miners. These developments were provided in small groups around Doncaster Road in Mexborough and around Low Road and Brook Square in Conisbrough. In 1905, one of the largest of these developments was provided on a site not far from the old village of Conisbrough, where a consortium of speculative builders led by local builder Messrs Earnshaw laid out 200 houses in Gardens Lane, Ivanhoe Road, Athelstane Road, Cadeby View and North Cliff Road, the latter street being originally known as Earnshaw's Lane after the aforementioned builder.

This postcard published by Walter Roelich c.1915 shows the villas constructed for colliery officials in Tickhill Square forming part of Phase 7. The houses feature bands of decorative brickwork, possibly the 'signature style' of local Conisbrough architect Harry Smethurst, and these bands can be seen at the level of the upper storey window sills. Harry Lawton Smethurst was responsible for designing most of the buildings constructed in Denaby Main from the early 1890s. He designed most of the colliery housing, the General and Mining Offices, the Denaby Main Hotel, All Saints Church, the Empire Cinema, and the Miners Welfare as well as housing for the Denaby Main Industrial & Co-operative Society and Kilner's Glassworks. Housing designed for other clients in the Conisbrough area also features this distinctive band of decorative brickwork. The building plans reproduced on the previous pages are unsigned but they may have been drawn by Harry Smethurst. Harry married Annie Kilner and inherited some of the Kilner's fortune on the death of Annie's father Caleb in 1920. Harry and Annie had a daughter Gwendoline, the grandmother of TV presenter Jeremy Clarkson.

Contrasts in housing at Denaby Main.

Above: *Villas provided for colliery management in Buckingham Road (Postcard by R. J. Rossor c1910).*
Below: *the backs of the houses in Loversall Street, showing the cramped conditions in the communal yards with the block of middens on the left. (Photographer unknown - Conisbrough & Denaby Main Heritage Collection)*

The Denaby Main Colliery Company was not the only organisation providing houses for their workforce, as, around 1900, the Denaby Main Industrial Co-operative Society purchased two plots of land from John Skipwith Herbert Fullerton of Thrybergh Hall, one to the east of Tickhill Street and another bounded by Tickhill Street, Hickleton Street, Bolton Street and Wheatley Street. A building application was made on 19th January 1901 and on the first plot they laid out 31 three bedroomed houses. These had blocks of land to the rear intended as communal gardens. On the second larger plot plans for 81 three bedroomed houses and a large communal garden were submitted but only 35 of these houses were ultimately constructed.

A 1910 postcard by R. J. Rossor showing Tickhill Street from the gates leading to the bowling green, tennis courts and cricket pitch in Tickhill Square. Much larger gates can be seen in an open position at the top of the street and their purpose remains unknown. These houses were designed by Harry Smethhurst and although officially built for the Denaby Main Industrial Co-operative Society, they were mostly used to house deputies at Denaby and Cadeby Main collieries. However, unlike the colliery housing, these houses were provided with small front gardens and a simple tiled porch above the front doors. Like much of the housing built in the period around 1900, it features a distinctive band of decorative brickwork carried between the levels of the adjacent window sills.

Coal Mining was not the only industry to come to Denaby in the 1860s. In 1865, Caleb Kilner leased an 11 acre site on Skitholme fields near Conisbrough Railway Station. On this site the Kilner family established Kilner's Provident Glassworks and built 24 cottages for their workforce with adjoining allotments and a large house as a family home. The firm was originally formed by John Kilner in 1844 who had opened his first glassworks in Castleford and a second glassworks in Dewsbury and who saw the benefits of a third site at Denaby due to its excellent transport links and ready supply of raw materials. John Kilner and his four sons named William, Caleb, George and John consequently developed the Denaby factory. Rather than using the name Denaby Main, Kilner's always referred to their factory and housing developments as being located in New Conisbrough.

George Kilner had a son, also called Caleb, and under their leadership the factory began to prosper. In 1895, they laid out a small housing development of 73 houses on Doncaster Road, opposite the colliery housing of Strafforth Terrace. On this site they built John Street, William Street, George Street, Thornhill Street and Lees Terrace, the streets taking their names from three of the brothers and the location of their main Dewsbury factory in Thornhill Lees. In 1902, George Kilner took up residence at Lowfield House whilst his son Caleb moved into Ivanhoe Lodge in Conisbrough which has been rebuilt from a smaller property in 1899.

In 1869 Kilner's Bridge was constructed across the railway line to provide access to their new development. The Provident Glassworks grew to employ 400 men and woman who produced beer and water bottles as well as the famous Kilner fruit preserving jar. This postcard by Walter Roelich, c 1915, shows the Prospect offices with some of the original housing dating from 1864 on the right. The private owner wagons on the left belong to Barber Walker's Bentley Colliery. (Norman Ellis Collection).

In 1905 the firm undertook further house building operations for their workforce in the Low Road area of Conisbrough. They laid out 127 houses and 2 shops in Castle Grove Terrace, Ferry Terrace, Ouse Terrace, Calder Terrace, Trent Terrace, Don Street, Dearne Street and Burcroft Hill. Most of these houses were built to designs by architect Harry Smethurst. In 1909, 14 larger properties known as Kimberley Cottage Villas were built in Low Road. In 1937, the Glassworks closed down and was subsequently demolished although the Prospect Offices were used by Amalgamated Denaby Collieries as additional offices.

In 1864, Denaby Pottery opened opposite the colliery and was worked by Williamson and Wardle from Staffordshire; it was the most easterly pottery in South Yorkshire. However, the venture was short lived and closed in 1870. The site subsequently became Samuel Meggitt's Mexborough Bone and Glue Works. In 1889, the Flameless Explosives Company commenced operations nearby for the manufacture of 'Securite', an explosive for use in the mining trade. The factory became known as the Powder Works and they provided a bowling green and tennis court for their employees. Like Kilner's Glassworks, the Powder Works provided an opportunity to employ female labour. The Powder works closed down in 1963 when they were absorbed as a department of Imperial Chemical Industries. Other employment opportunities were provided by the limestone quarries at Cadeby, and other industries at Conisbrough, including the brickworks, the Sickle Works, the Fat Refinery and Holywell Brewery.

The construction of an entirely new settlement with a large population meant that a whole host of services would be needed in the form of shops, schools, places of worship, pubs and clubs, together with sporting and leisure facilities and transport connections to surrounding towns. The earliest shops were opened in some of the front rooms of the original Pit Row houses in the late 1860s together with a row of purpose built wooden shops located on the opposite side of Doncaster Road. Over the level crossing, a small wooden shop stood opposite the pit gates and was maintained by Mr and Mrs Kane to provide the miners with pop and chewing tobacco and cigarettes for when they came off shift. The cigarettes were sold individually and were lit by a large candle on the shop counter thus saving the cost of matches!

With the opening of the second phase of the colliery housing in 1882, the colliery company opened the Denaby Main Stores on Melton View. However, this venture was not successful and in 1883 the stores were enlarged with a grocery and beer off license and converted into the Denaby Main Industrial & Co-operative Society. The Co-operative Society subsequently opened branches on Hickleton Street (1908), Strafforth Terrace (1913), Doncaster Road (1948) and School Walk

(1951). The original Co-operative building housed the first village post office before the post office moved to purpose built premises in Wood View in 1892.

Some of the buildings fronting Doncaster Road also opened as shops whilst private builders provided additional blocks of purpose built shops known as Wray's Buildings, Central Buildings, Princess Buildings and Alexander Buildings. Next to the Denaby Main Hotel, the Denaby Main Market Hall opened until it was replaced by a purpose built Market Place in Church Road in 1931. There were other shops scattered throughout the village including Booths Fish and Chip Shop on Annerley Street and three pawnbrokers on Doncaster Road. The village shops and the various mobile traders could supply the village with all their requirements and there was little need to shop in adjoining towns.

This row of wooden shops was located on the northern side of Doncaster Road at the eastern end of Pit Row and was built around 1905. In the distance across the railway can be seen the Luhrig Coal Washing Plant at Denaby Main Colliery. In the centre are the Central Cash Stores belonging to W. J. Parkes with next door, Mr Gibson, trading as the Denaby Main Newsagent and Chocolate Box Shop. Mr Gibson had another shop near the Denaby Main Hotel. Finally on the right T. Anthony was a General dealer of Tobacco. Note the advertising signs for Rowntree's Chocolates and Fry's Chocolates, a sweet treat for many children in the village. (Postcard c.1915 by Walter Roelich)

The 1870 Education Act had set the framework for the compulsory schooling of all children aged from 5 to 13 and in that year Thomas Gray Fullerton of

Thrybergh Hall opened a Church School in Old Denaby although Denaby Main children were generally not permitted to attend this school. Consequently, in 1872 the colliery company built the pit school to the rear of Pit Row in Doncaster Road. They provided the building and employed the teaching staff directly in exchange for government grants and payments for the education of the children. With the expansion of the village in the 1880s the school became overcrowded and in 1883 the colliery company provided a new Boys' and Girls' School in Rossington Street with the infants remaining in the earlier school.

The Denaby Main Ambulance Band are seen here in front of the main entrance to the Church School or Large Hall School in Rossington Street. The lintel over the door bears the inscription 'Denaby Main Colliery School 1893' reflecting the influence of the colliery company in providing education for the children of the village. In 1902, the West Riding County Council took over administration of the school although the colliery company remained as managers and provided money for maintenance. The school was demolished in 2001 having been replaced with new premises on an adjacent site. (Andrew McGarrigle Collection).

The School Inspectorate were still not satisfied with the educational provision and, with a rapidly increasing population, in the early 1890s, Mr Chambers instigated plans for a much larger school under the management of the colliery company in Rossington Street on a site donated by Andrew Montagu of Melton Park. This was initially known as the Church School and was built by the colliery at a cost of £5,000 to educate the children during the day and act as a church on Sundays; it contained a large hall with a capacity of 1,000 to provide an entertainment venue and cultural centre in the evenings. The Church School was opened by the Archbishop of York on 23rd October 1893 and subsequently became known as the Large Hall School. The original school on Doncaster Road closed down and the 400 boys were housed in the school built in 1883 and the Large Hall School accommodated 1,000 girls and infants. In 1932 the Boy's School burnt down and the boys moved into the Large Hall School.

On 30th March 1911 another school opened at the top of Balby Street at a cost of £7,000 on a site donated by Frederick Montague of Melton Park. This school was known as the Mixed Council School with accommodation for 600 children. This passed into the ownership of West Riding County Council in 1935 and was renamed Balby Street County Primary School. It eventually closed in 1986 and was demolished, although the two school towers were left to provide a landmark before being demolished to make way for new housing in 2015. The West Riding County Council provided another school near Conisbrough Railway Station which opened as Station Road School in 1913 or 1914. This school was mostly used by children from the Burcroft areas although several Denaby families, particularly those living in the eastern side of the village, sent their children to Station Road School. On 1st October 1926, the Roman Catholics opened their own school on Wadworth Street on a site donated by Frederick Montagu of Melton Park.

Religious worship was first conducted in one of the former barns adjacent to the Reresby Arms by the Reverend Henry Ellershaw of Mexborough Church. In 1891 the barn was converted into St Chad's Church when Denaby Parish became a conventional parish independent of Mexborough Parish. Services were also conducted in the Rossington Street Church School from 1893, but it was clear that the community desired a purpose built church. A site for a new church was donated by Andrew Montagu and his nephew Frederick Montagu contributed £1,000 towards the cost of construction, with the Alfred Marriott bequest charity donating £15,000. There were further donations from Kilner's Glassworks and the colliery company agreed to pay the stipend. Attached to the church was a large vicarage with accommodation for a vicar and curate, with a church hall constructed across the road in Church Walk. The whole project was opened by the Archbishop of York on 21st September 1900. With the opening of All Saints Church, St Chad's Church became a Sunday School, with an additional Sunday school opening in Blythe Street, which was known as St Chad's Mission Hall. In 1975, All Saints Church was demolished and replaced with a new church across the road next to the church hall with the Miners Memorial Chapel opening in 1987.

The architects of All Saints' Church were Hodgson Fowler and Harry Smethurst and the building was constructed by B. Wortley of Doncaster from local sandstone quarried nearby at Mexborough and Hooton Roberts although the quoins were of Ancaster limestone from Lincolnshire. This postcard by James Simonton c.1915 shows the church, described as 'dull' by Nikolaus Pevsner in the 'Yorkshire West Riding' volume of his landmark work: 'The Buildings of England'. (Andrew McGarrigle Collection).

Prior to 1894, the Roman Catholics of the village had to attend services in Wath or Doncaster, but in that year the colliery company invited Father Kavanagh to develop a Catholic community in the village and they provided him with a house and placed the old school in Doncaster Road at his disposal for services. Andrew Montagu of Melton Park donated a large plot of land for the Roman Catholic Community to establish a church, school, club and convent. Under the dynamic leadership of Father Kavanagh, £4,000 was successfully raised to build a church and on 18th October 1897 the foundation stone of St Alban's Church was laid by Bishop Gordon of Leeds. Bishop Gordon returned to perform the first mass at the church on 22nd June 1898.

In 1891, the Wesleyan Methodists were given a site on Doncaster Road by Andrew Montagu of Melton Park and on 15th June 1891 they laid the foundation stones for the Epworth Hall, constructed at a cost of £1,524. A wooden hut behind the chapel served as a Sunday school until this was replaced with a permanent structure in 1924. The Wesleyan Chapel ceased to be a place of worship in 1974 and the premises were taken over by Reg Elliff who used the building to house a photographic laboratory. After standing derelict for many years the chapel was demolished in 2009. The Primitive Methodist's established Lowfield Chapel on

Doncaster Road in 1895, which closed in 1968 with the building being converted for industrial use. The Baptist church opened on the junction of Doncaster Road and Balby Street in 1902 but closed in 1920. The building was subsequently purchased by the colliery company who converted it into the Denaby Main Officials Club. The Salvation Army first met in the old Doncaster Road School in 1893 before moving to their present citadel in School Walk in 1928.

A postcard by an unknown photographer featuring the Roman Catholic Church and Presbytery at Denaby Main. The bell tower was added in 1910 and the north aisle and Sacred Heart Chapel were built in 1911. St Alban's Institute opened in 1923 with St Alban's School following in 1926; the Convent of Mercy opened next to the church in 1927. (John Petch Collection).

During the nineteenth century, local hospital provision was provided by various trusts and charities. Anyone who sustained injuries or suffered from illness was usually treated at home, although in serious cases, the patient would be transported by horse and cart to Doncaster Hospital. At the time there were no sick pay benefits; therefore any absence from work went unpaid. Nevertheless, in areas where a high percentage of the workforce was employed in potentially dangerous occupations, cottage hospitals were often established to provide free treatment paid for by weekly contributions deducted from the workers' pay. In 1890, the Montagu Cottage Hospital had opened in Mexborough but this was deemed inadequate to serve the growing population of Denaby Main.

Consequently, on September 1903, a public meeting was held in Rossington Street School with the aim of establishing and maintaining a cottage hospital for the workmen employed at Denaby and Cadeby Collieries. John Skipwith Herbert Fullerton donated a site at the top of Stainton Street and in 1905 a new hospital opened at a cost of £3,000 under the name Fullerton Hospital. One of the first doctors was Doctor John MacArthur who later lived in Red House in Tickhill Square. There was also a Doctor's surgery in Annerley Street and in 1938, the West Riding County Council opened a clinic in Church Road. Fullerton Hospital passed into the ownership of the National Health Service in 1947 and was closed in 1989, the building subsequently becoming a school for children with special educational needs. A rapidly increasing population naturally meant that deaths were now a common occurrence and in the 1890s John Fullerton gifted a plot of land for use as a cemetery. This was extended and subsequently run by Conisbrough Urban District Council who built a house to accommodate the grave digger.

The Reresby Arms on Doncaster Road, located opposite Pit Row, (part of the first phase of colliery housing developed from 1868). Above the door can be seen the Reresby coat of arms which featured a boar above its shield. This led to the establishment becoming universally referred to as 'The Pig'. The pub was immensely successful, ideally positioned to slake the men's thirst as they came off shift at Denaby Colliery located by the level crossing in the distance. Initially, the Reresby Arms remained in the ownership of the Fullerton family and was run by tenants but it subsequently passed to Ind Coope & Company, the Burton-on-Trent brewers. It was latterly known as The Milestone and was demolished in 2008. (Postcard by Walter Roelich, c.1915)

In 1869 the old farm opposite Pit Row was restructured as a refreshment house which was subsequently licensed to sell alcohol from 1877. It was initially known as the Fullerton Arms but was renamed as the Reresby Arms after the Sir John Reresby who originally owned the manor of Denaby before it was inherited by Colonel John Fullerton.

Aware of the large profits made at the Reresby Arms, the Denaby Main Colliery Company decided to provide their own rival licensed premises and in 1894 they opened the Denaby Main Hotel, designed by Harry Smethhurst. This new establishment was located at the other end of the village, ideally situated to quench the appetite of men coming off shift at Cadeby Main Colliery. The Denaby Main Hotel was run directly by the colliery company and was always known as 'The Drum' by the men. It was originally run by a staff of 10, all servants of the colliery company, and had stables to the rear and rooms upstairs for visitors. In 1896 it was extended with the addition of a large tap room or 'boozy' with a concert hall and billiard room.

The Denaby Main Hotel opened for business in 1894 and was run by the colliery company themselves until 1927 when they sold the establishment to the Sheffield brewery, Duncan Gilmour & Company. This postcard by R. J. Rossor, c1910, also features David Haigh's pawnbrokers business on the left, indicated by the distinctive three golden balls attached to the outside of the building, with another pawnbrokers visible in the distance occupying part of Princess's Buildings. (Norman Ellis Collection).

The colliery company built the Denaby Main Institute on Annerley Street which was opened by Richard Pope in 1873 and run by a committee of colliery officials in order to provide leisure facilities for their workforce who could join as members. The building contained a billiard room, bagatelle room and reading room with a supply of books and newspapers, and was licensed to sell draught beer for consumption on the premises.

The institute was always referred to as 'the Stute' and was later extended with the addition of another billiard room and an Assembly Room, which was used for mining classes, lectures, wedding receptions and parties. The institute took over the old school in Doncaster Road for a few years from 1891 and converted it into a gymnasium but this appears to have been little used. From 1890 the Denaby Main Colliery Brass band was based at the institute and the library was greatly expanded in conjunction with the Denaby Main Industrial Co-operative Society. The institute closed in 1971 with the redevelopment of the colliery village and moved into newly built premises on Bolton Street.

Other Working Men's clubs were established in the village. In 1919 the Denaby Comrades Club was established in Rossington Street by men returning from the First World War. The initial premises were a tin hut which was replaced with a permanent structure in 1926 when the club became part of the British Legion. The Denaby and Cadeby Officials club opened in 1922 using the former Baptist Chapel that had closed in 1920. Further along Doncaster Road, the North Cliff Working Men's Club opened in 1921 followed by St Alban's Institute & Club next to the Roman Catholic Church in 1923. The Labour Club was established in Central Buildings on Doncaster Road, but turned out to be short lived as the premises were subsequently used by David Haigh's pawnbrokers

In 1919 at the annual meeting of the Denaby Main Institute, Mr Chambers stated that the company would be willing to provide £5,000 for a new building to include extensive recreational facilities. As it was, the establishment of the Mining Industry Act (1920) saw the formation of the British Miners' Welfare Fund whose purpose was to improve the social well-being, recreation and general conditions in the country's coalfields, funded by a levy of a penny on every ton of coal produced. In 1922 a scheme was drawn up for the construction of the Denaby Main Miners Welfare on a site in Tickhill Square donated by the colliery company and located between the football and cricket pitches. With a grant of £20,000 from the fund, the building was designed by Harry Smethhurst and built by William Robinson of Sheffield. The Miner's Welfare was opened in 1924 by Herbert Smith, the president of the Miners Federation of Great Britain, and consisted of a lecture hall, sporting facilities, 'educational and fictional libraries', billiards rooms, smoke rooms, slipper baths and a large swimming pool. It was intended that the new facilities would be used by all the miners and their families with running costs drawn by a weekly wage deduction from those that became members. In 1964, the library moved to a new building opened by West Riding County Council in Church Road.

Postcard publisher Edgar Scrivens recorded this view of the swimming baths in the Miners Welfare. The baths could be covered over and used as a gymnasium, and gymnastic training rings can be seen on the right. On 8th October 1910, the colliery company opened a small recreational area near Cliff View which included the provision of open air swimming baths, which were reserved for the use of men only. The operation of the open air baths passed to Conisbrough Urban District Council in 1921 and were closed in 1930 following the opening of the covered baths at the Miners Welfare. These swimming baths later closed and were replaced with facilities at the new Dearne Valley Leisure Centre built on the site of Denaby Main Colliery.

Colliery communities are well known for their interest in sporting activities and Denaby Main was no exception. In 1878, the Denaby Cricket Club was formed, initially playing on a pitch near Church Walk. In 1900 they moved to new pitch in Tickhill Square. They also built a wooden pavilion which was replaced in 1930 with a permanent brick built structure. Established in 1895 as Denaby Church Football Club and renamed Denaby United Football Club in 1898, the football club first played on a ground behind the Reresby Arms but in 1902 they moved to a new pitch on Tickhill Square and joined the Midland League. A stand was built in Tickhill Square and the club regularly drew large attendances to its home games, recording a record attendance of 5,200 in 1927 for a FA Cup first round match against Southport Football Club. In 2001 the Denaby & Cadeby Miners Welfare trustees wished to open the pitch to community use and this unfortunately led to the dissolution of the club and they were wound up in 2002. However, in 2011 Denaby United reformed playing from the Old Road Recreational Fields at Conisbrough.

Tickhill Square was also the home to the Denaby and Cadeby Tennis Club which was formed in 1907 and was provided with two courts near the Official's houses. In 1909, a bowls club was established with two greens in Tickhill Square. In 1920 a Rifle Club was started by ex-servicemen returning from the First World War in premises next to the Comrades Club in Rossington Street. The Comrades Club also provided facilities for a boxing club, although unofficial bare knuckle boxing matches had been held on Denaby Crags for many years. The boxing club later transferred to Tickhill Square with the opening of the Tom Hill Youth Centre in 1949. Other clubs included the Cycling Club, the Fishing Club and various allotment societies.

The Scouts met in a scout hut on Kirby's Hill (the lower end of Bolton Street) and in 1909 a Girls Institute opened in Cliff View. This was later used by the St John's Ambulance Brigade and was known as the 'blood and bandage'. That year also saw the opening of a drill hall on Doncaster Road which was used by cadets from the King's Own Yorkshire Light Infantry.

In 1931, a £2,000 project was drawn up by Conisbrough Urban District Council to provide a park in the centre of the village next to the new market. Frederick Montagu donated a site on Doncaster Road and in 1932 the Memorial Park opened, as captured in this postcard by James Simonton published in the 1930s. In the distance can be seen the houses of the Conanby Avenues estate, complete with the smoking boiler house chimney which provided these dwellings with an unlimited hot water supply. In November 8th 1953 a cenotaph was unveiled in the park and much later a bandstand was added.

With no gardens provided for the houses, the village was surrounded by numerous allotments, which were used for vegetable and flower growing, and the keeping of pigs, poultry and foul. Many men were keen pigeon racers and kept a pigeon shed. In the early days, opportunities for leisure were minimum and Sundays were typically spent walking in the local area, with walks to Old Denaby and down the River Don to Levitt Hagg and Sprotbrough proving popular. There were tea rooms at Conisbrough and by Conisbrough Locks where rowing boats could be hired. Viner's Pond had been created by the truncation of a meander in the River Don by the railway in 1849 and was a popular venue for fishing. An annual treat was a visit to Ticklecock Fair at Conisbrough which attracted numerous visitors from the surrounding districts. Most of the clubs and church groups ran annual day trips to the coast for their members in the summer, usually departing by chartered train from Conisbrough Railway Station or by a fleet of buses. These trips were extremely popular and provided a day away at the coast at places like Cleethorpes, Blackpool or Bridlington.

On a site near Tickhill Square, the Miners Welfare and local council opened the 'Swing Park' in 1932, a children's park equipped with swings, slides, roundabouts and popular rocking features known as 'Witches' Hats'. The Swing Park proved very popular but was eventually closed during the 1960s and buried beneath a landfill site. In the distance the ground rises steeply forming North Cliff and Denaby Crags. This area of rough pasture and limestone rock outcrops became an informal adventure playground for the children of the village, although at the time of writing the crags are being slowly colonised by woodland. The identity of the four children is unknown, as is the photographer who recorded this view, possibly in the 1940s. (Conisbrough & Denaby Main Heritage Group Collection)

In 1913, the Denaby Empire Picture House, built to a design by Harry Smethhurst, opened on Doncaster Road. This handsome building was constructed from brick and fronted with stucco and terracotta. Unfortunately, on the opening night of 3rd November 1913, the crowd of 2,500 had to be turned away as the cinema had not obtained a license in time. However, on the following evening, a crowd of 1,200 were entertained to a triple bill of silent movies, including one with local connections: *Ivanhoe*, directed by Herbert Brenon. The cinema proved tremendously popular and frequently played to full houses at the weekend, with Saturday mornings being reserved for the 'penny rush' when children from the area would rush to matinee showings paying a penny to enjoy a programme of cartoons and serials. With changing tastes, the building eventually closed in 1962 and reopened as a bingo hall and is currently a gymnasium and fitness centre.

This postcard by Edgar Scrivens taken in the early 1930s is titled Main Street but actually depicts Doncaster Road looking towards Mexborough with the Empire Cinema in the centre and with trolleybus wires overhead. On the left is Clifton Street, as indicated by the road name sign affixed to the house. The doors of many of the colliery owned properties were often painted dark green with cream windowsills. On the right, Central Garage opened in 1928 as the village's first petrol station with Lowfield House beyond being the home of George Kilner. This became the Police Station belonging to the West Riding Constabulary in 1935. In the far distance can be seen the Primitive Methodist's Lowfield Chapel with a gantry of railway signals guarding the entrance to Lowfield Junction where the colliery company's South Yorkshire Junction Railway commenced. (Postcard by Edgar Scrivens, John Petch Collection).

Denaby Main had excellent transport links which was one of the reasons why the colliery company and the glassworks had chosen the area. The South Yorkshire Railway opened in 1849 and a railway station was opened at Conisbrough, which was subsequently rebuilt and enlarged in 1884. The South Yorkshire Railway became part of the Manchester, Sheffield and Lincolnshire Railway and were subsequently renamed the Great Central Railway in 1897. The line crossed the Doncaster Road on a level crossing and in 1850 a signal box and gate house was provided for railway employees; the signal box became known as Denaby Crossing although the area was always referred to as 'the crossings'. With increasing road traffic and a very busy main line with frequent passenger trains and numerous freight trains, the crossings became renowned for notorious delays. A pedestrian footbridge was provided which proved an ideal vantage point for transport photographers to capture road and rail transport over the years prior to its dismantling in 1980 although it was not to be until 2004 with the opening of Bambury Bridge that delays for road traffic at the crossings became a thing of the past. The majority of the coal was dispatched by rail along the Great Central Railway, the Dearne Valley Railway and the Company's own South Yorkshire Junction Railway which linked to the Hull and Barnsley Railway.

Dating from 1915 and published by James Simonton & Sons, this postcard depicts a freight train rumbling through Conisbrough Railway Station with Cadeby Main Colliery beyond and was photographed from Kilner's Bridge which provided road and pedestrian access to the colliery and the glassworks. An additional pedestrian access was also provided by extending the railway station footbridge over a freight bypass line as shown in the distance. The building in the centre is Cadeby Villas, one of which was the home of the colliery manager. This building was later used as the colliery wages office.

From 1880, the colliery company took delivery of several standard gauge steam locomotives to perform shunting duties and over the following years they purchased locomotives named BUCKINGHAM, MELTON, CLIFTON, SPROTBRO, CONISBRO, WARMSWORTH, DENABY, THRYBERGH, RERESBY, a second loco named SPROTBROUGH and finally ABERCONWAY. These were all named after local villages apart from BUCKINGHAM which was named after John Buckingham Pope and ABERCONWAY, named after Lord Aberconway, the YAC Chairman. In 1900, the company took delivery of four locomotives built to higher specifications for working on the mainline railway network. These locos were named DENABY, CADEBY, MELTON and FIRSBY and they were employed on duties shuttling rakes of coal wagons along the Great Central Railway to Hexthorpe yard near Doncaster where the wagons were marshalled for onward transport to the London market via the Great Northern Railway. To house their fleet of locomotives, the colliery company constructed a loco shed at Denaby Main Colliery with a smaller shed adjacent to Cadeby Main Colliery.

By 1751, the River Don had been made navigable from the River Humber to Tinsley near Sheffield with occasional canal cuts with locks provided to bypass the weirs on the river. Consequently coal staithes were positioned on the river by the colliery company and coal was dispatched by boat to Doncaster Gas Works and the Power Stations at Doncaster, Rotherham and Blackburn Meadows near Sheffield, as well as for export via Goole Docks, with the last coal sent by boat in 1981. Incidentally, when Mexborough Power Station opened in 1952 on a site near the colliery adjacent to the canal, it would never receive coal by boat, being supplied by rail until its closure in the 1980s. Adjacent to the River Don, the colliery opened up a land sale yard with coal loading chutes to load coal, initially into horse drawn carts for local sale in the area. Another land sale yard was provided near Lowfield Junction. In 1919, the Denaby and Cadeby Home Coal Carting Committee was established from a base in the stables of Ferry Farm in Conisbrough and undertook the task of delivering the miners' monthly concessionary coal allowance.

Prior to 1907, most people travelled to the adjoining towns on foot or by carrier's cart, typically to Doncaster Market for the day. In 1907, the Mexborough & Swinton Tramways Company opened a lengthy street tramway from Rotherham to a terminus at Denaby Toll Bar, as the narrow hump backed bridge over the canal had prohibited any further expansion into Denaby Main. On 31st August 1915, Mexborough & Swinton introduced two feeder routes using rail-less traction vehicles or trolleybuses. The first route connected Mexborough with Manvers Main Colliery whilst the other connected Denaby Toll Bar with Conisbrough and ran along Doncaster Road through the village to terminate at the junction of Station Road and Elm Green Lane not far from Conisbrough Castle and outside The Laurels, the home of William Chambers. In 1928 the trams were withdrawn and the two trolleybus routes were linked to operate from Manvers Main Colliery through Mexborough and Denaby with an extension along Conisbrough High Street to terminate at the new colliery housing estate in Conanby in 1929; this service was known as Conisbrough High. A new branch left the line at Conisbrough Railway Station to run along Low Road to terminate at Brook Square adjacent to Conisbrough Brickworks and this service was known as Conisbrough Low and trolleybuses departing from this terminus worked over the full length of the former tram route to Rotherham. Larger trackless vehicles were now employed as the canal bridge at Denaby Toll Bar had been rebuilt and the Mexborough & Swinton 'tracklessess' would provide a frequent service from Conisbrough via Denaby Main to Rotherham.

One of the early Mexborough & Swinton Traction Company's rail-less electric vehicles photographed when newly delivered in 1922 on Doncaster Road alongside the houses of Pit Row with Denaby Main Colliery in the background. This vehicle was an AEC Model 602 with Strachan Brown bodywork for 36 passengers. It gained electrical power from the overhead wiring and with its solid rubber tyres, must have given a somewhat bumpy ride on the roads of the day. Initially, trolleybuses were not obliged to display registrations at the front of the vehicle, although this example is likely to be WY 3059 and numbered 26 in the Mexborough & Swinton fleet. The initial livery was red and cream although in post-war years the tracklesses were painted in a distinctive green and cream colour scheme. Note the advertising hoardings displaying the programme at the Grand Theatre in Doncaster where the Four K-Foleys were providing entertainment, whilst the Denaby Empire was screening a trio of silent movies including Civilian Clothes, directed by Hugh Ford in 1920. (Paul Fox Collection).

Motor bus services came to Denaby Main in 1919 when the Barnsley and District Traction Company introduced a Barnsley – Mexborough –Doncaster service using light weight vehicles able to pass the 5 ton weight limit on the canal bridge at Denaby Toll Bar. A rival service introduced by James Guest of Swinton from Kilnhurst to Doncaster was taken over by Barnsley and District in 1928 when they were renamed Yorkshire Traction and they eventually absorbed the Mexborough & Swinton Company in 1969.

By the mid-1890s with the opening of Cadeby Main Colliery, over 1,000 colliery houses had been built in Denaby Main, all at around the cost of £50 per house and at a density of 49 to the acre - it was said that two keys opened most of the front doors in the village. The houses had been provided cheaply with the most basic of facilities. There were no gardens or private back yards; instead there were large communal yards called 'the backs' containing blocks of middens, and water for the whole village was supplied by two standpipes. The area was dominated by life at the two pits and every house had a coal fire which was lighted most days, consequently blanketing the area under a haze of smoke with soot and grime coating the walls of the houses. Despite this, the miners wives worked hard to keep their houses clean and Mondays would always be washdays when clothes were put out to dry in the backs. However, some of the houses were infested with bugs and cockroaches or 'blackcocks' as they were known. Indeed one former miner told me that as a child living in one of the old houses, he once chased one of the blackcocks up the wall with a candle, but the bug was so large that it turned round and blew the candle out!

Needless to say, sanitary conditions were poor and disease was commonplace with frequent outbreaks of typhoid and scarlet fever, all probably contributed to by the insufficient water supply and the unsanitary state of the middens. Most of the houses were overcrowded and the high birth rate was matched with a high infant mortality rate of 220 per 1000, possibly one of the highest rates in the country at the time. The men were paid their weekly wage on Friday and, as mining was thirsty work and notoriously dangerous with the ever threat of injury or death, many of them 'lived for the day' and spent most of their wages on heavy drinking sessions, gambling and playing 'pitch and toss' in the streets. Any money left was used to retrieve the families' possessions from the pawnbrokers, pay off the weekly slate at the local shops and barter with the mobile traders and various peddlers and street hawkers who would visit the area.

On 8th November 1899, Denaby Main would gain national notoriety throughout the country when *The Christian Budget*, a Christian journal promoting Christian beliefs, labelled the village as being "the worst in England" and "a hell upon

Earth". The Special Correspondent for the *Christian Budget* wrote a two page article deriding the community for its reliance upon drinking, betting, gambling, swearing and the general conduct of the men, women and children stating that on Saturday evening the place is like a pandemonium. The article concluded with a paragraph entitled "Where are the churches?

Naturally there was an outcry amongst the community over the publication and the colliery company successfully brought legal proceedings against the publishers, forcing them to make a public apology and the colliery company pointed out the good work of the Denaby Main Institute, the churches, community groups, clubs and societies. An example of this was provided by Caleb Kilner: when speaking at a bazaar held to raise funds for the Wesleyan Methodist Chapel, he stated that Denaby Main had been stigmatised as the worst village in England and that this statement had travelled the length and breadth of the country, but he doubted that the news of the successful fundraising bazaar in the so called worst village in England would also travel the length and breadth of the country.

It was obvious that the *Christian Budget* article greatly over exaggerated the problems experienced in the village; however, it is probably fair to say that the village was not built to the standards that the colliery company claimed it to be. Whilst they had been generous on one hand with the provision of housing, schools, churches, institutes and support for numerous clubs and societies, on the other hand, their pursuit of profits had gained them a reputation for ruthless efficiency and they employed an almost despotic power over the village, frequently using the power of eviction during periods of industrial conflict to keep the workforce subdued. Is it possible that these powers maybe contributed to some of the scenes witnessed by the *Christian Budget's* special correspondent? As it was, a conference held at Doncaster Mansion House to discuss the provision of colliery housing in South Yorkshire condemned the housing provided at Denaby Main as being "long rows of monotonous ugliness" and this led to noted town planner Patrick Abercrombie producing the Doncaster Regional Planning Scheme in 1922.

Nevertheless, conditions began to improve with all of the housing being finally connected with fresh water and all new housing built from 1902 provided with outside toilets instead of unsanitary middens. Since 1878, the housing had been supplied with gas from the colliery gasworks and from 1902 they were all provided with a cold water supply. However, the middens continued to be used by those living in the pre-1900 houses until 1923 when a scheme was implemented to replace them with individual water closets built onto the rear of the properties. The project, funded by the Ministry of Health and Conisbrough Urban District Council, saw toilets installed at 1,210 properties in Denaby Main and New

Conisbrough and 690 in the older houses and cottages of Conisbrough village. As part of this scheme, the houses in Denaby Main were connected to the sewer network and the sewage works on Denaby Lane opened in 1926. Finally, between 1938 and 1940, Amalgamated Denaby Collieries spent £500,000 in improvements to the quality of the colliery housing.

The development of the Parkgate coal seam at Denaby and Cadeby Main Collieries in the 1920s brought the need to employ more men and consequently the colliery company decided to implement a new housing scheme to provide accommodation for 400 families. This time an elevated site on the plateau above Denaby Crags was chosen and to take advantage of Government grants and loans initiated under the Housing Act (1919) in order to build housing to a higher standard to meet qualities imposed by the Ministry of Health, it was necessary to form a public utility society.

Therefore the colliery company formed a separate subsidiary, the Conisbrough Housing Association Ltd. to construct this new development. Under the scheme, the Public Works Loan Board would provide a loan to cover 2/3 of the cost of the development and provide a subsidy for every house constructed. The colliery company architect, Harry Smethurst, remained as Secretary to the Conisbrough Housing Association, but they commissioned the Architectural Town Planning Association Ltd. of 31 Grosvenor Place, London, to design the houses in pairs and blocks of 4 and 6 as well as laying out the streets and grounds with the houses laid out at a density of no more than 10 per acre.

An 80 acre site was purchased from the Countess of Yarborough and considerable thought was given to the planning of the new estate with the use of wide avenues and green verges and extensive front and back gardens. The houses were of a number of different varieties to suit differing family requirements, but typically had three or four bedrooms upstairs and a living room, kitchen, bathroom and toilet downstairs; the idea being that men coming off shift in their dirty clothes could head straight into the downstairs bathroom without disturbing the rest of the house, as this was well before the widespread introduction of pithead baths. In 1924, the builders A. Bull & Company of Thurnscoe commenced work on the site. Space was left for a recreation ground and an open green area at the front of the development which it was hoped would form a terminus for an extension to the local trolleybus system. Another space was left for the provision of shops to be erected by private enterprise but subject to the approval of the colliery company. The initial plan was for 400 houses with space for 400 more if needed.

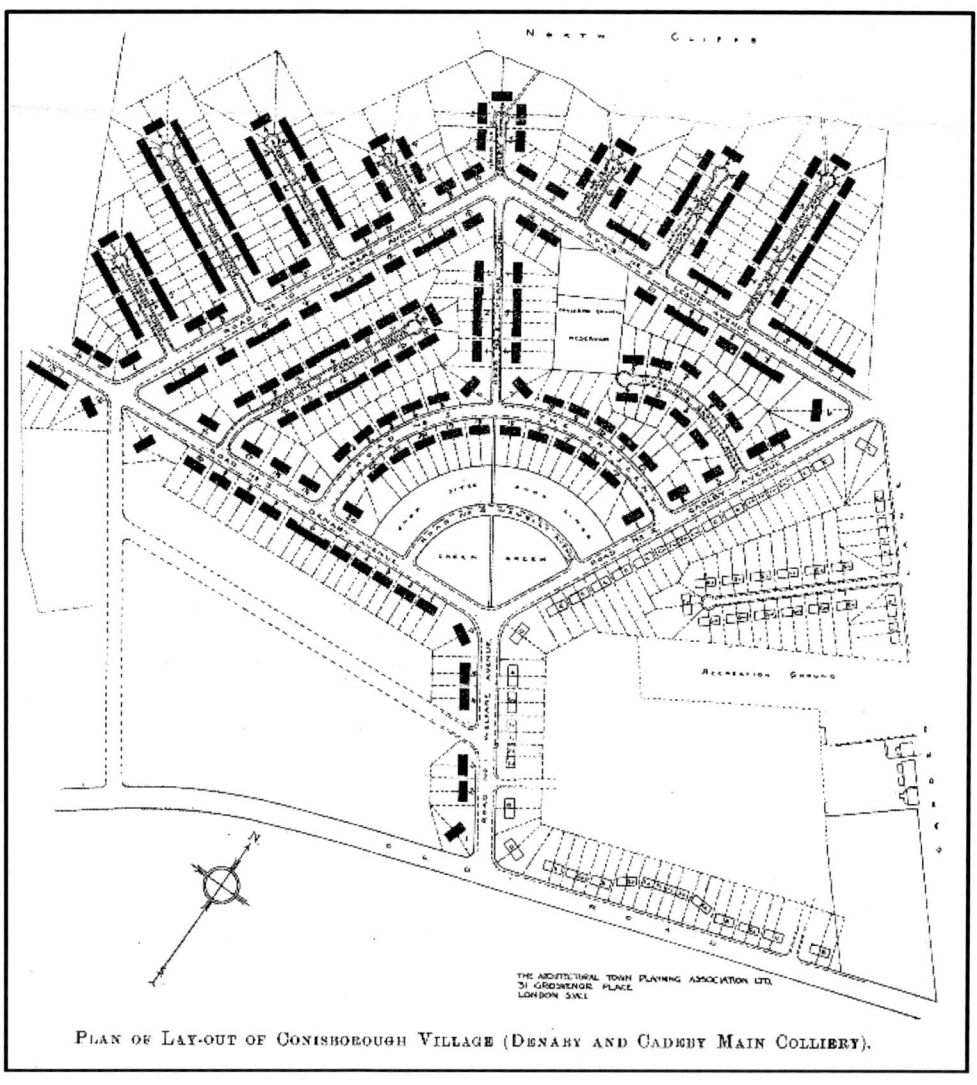

PLAN OF LAY-OUT OF CONISBOROUGH VILLAGE (DENABY AND CADEBY MAIN COLLIERY).

Layout plan of what was originally known as the Conisbrough Village estate. The scheme called for 400 houses (shaded black - with space for an additional 400 – 100 of which are depicted unshaded), together with a recreation ground and a green forming an entrance to the estate at the top of Welfare Avenue. Note the other proposed avenues, one parallel with Denaby Avenue and the other connecting Chambers Avenue to Old Road. With building developments provided by Conisbrough Urban District Council to the south of Old Road, it was decided not to complete the additional 400 houses. The initial batch of 400 houses had been built at a cost of £225,000 or around £562 each and were all occupied by 1926. (Colliery Guardian).

The domestic water supply for the whole of Denaby and Conisbrough was supplied from the North Cliff Reservoir, itself fed by water pumped up from the borehole at Cadeby Main Colliery and this water source would supply the new development. However, it was intended to supply the new houses with an unlimited supply of hot water heated by a coal fired boiler house built at a cost of £14,000. Next to the boiler house, a colliery home repairs office was built to serve the houses. The boiler house provided hot and cold water to supply the baths, sinks and lavatories in the new houses. Hot water was conveyed from the boiler house by means of a 6 mile long pipe which connected all the houses and entered them between the ground and first floors. With a continuous supply of hot water it was hoped that this would reduce the need for the use of domestic fires during the warmer weather and be of greater convenience for domestic uses in the home, resulting in a cleaner environment as one chimney at the boiler house would replace 400 individual chimneys. The hot water supply was indeed a novel feature for the time although it was often said that it would run cold at times of high demand, especially if your house was towards the end of the 6 mile long pipe! Nevertheless, the provision of hot water was a huge benefit especially as at the time it was traditional for the men to clean themselves in a zinc bath in front of the open fire with hot water carried in from copper in the kitchen.

The streets were all given names connected with the colliery. The main entrance to the estate from Old Road was named Welfare Road to reflect the importance of the Miners Welfare Fund which had just provided a Miners Welfare in Denaby Main and would provide a recreational ground and pavilion for the men of Conisbrough on Gardens Lane in 1928. The Crescent connected Denaby Avenue and Cadeby Avenue, named after the two collieries. An area for shops was allocated along Wembley Avenue, named after the Wembley Exhibition of 1924. Barnsley Avenue and Parkgate Avenue were named after the two main coal seams mined at the pits. Leslie Avenue, Peake Avenue, Chambers Avenue were named after the new colliery managing director, chairman, and former managing director respectively whilst Pope Avenue was named after the three generations of the Pope family that had run the colliery company up to 1923. Washington Avenue was named after the subsidiary Washington Colliery located in County Durham. The owners of the major coal royalties were represented with Fullerton Avenue (Thrybergh Hall), Fitzwilliam Avenue (Earl Fitzwilliam's Hooton Roberts estate), Copley Avenue (Sprotbrough Hall) and Montagu Avenue (Melton Park), Finally Halifax Avenue was named after the Viscount Halifax of Hickleton Hall, trustee of the Cadeby Main Disaster Relief Fund. The final street was named Markham Avenue after the Markham family. The Markhams had no directorial connections with Denaby and Cadeby Collieries, although Arthur Markham and Charlie Markham had been the Chairmen of the neighbouring collieries at Brodsworth and Edlington to which Cadeby Colliery had subleased some of their seams. The colliery company numbered the houses with green numbers on a cream background positioned next to the front doors.

HOUSES IN THE CRESCENT, CONISBOROUGH.
(Pipes for the central heating scheme may be seen between the houses.

BLOCK OF FOUR HOUSES, TYPES E AND F, AT CONISBOROUGH.

MONTAGU AVENUE, CONISBOROUGH.

Newly completed houses in the Avenues estate in 1925. The houses were all originally designated by letter according to their architectural style, for example Type A, Type B, Type C etc. Montagu Avenue is now known as Montague Avenue. (Colliery Guardian)

The new estate was officially referred to as the Avenues estate but was often called Chinatown, due to the fact that many of the new families who came to live in the area had come from the Staffordshire China Potteries. From its high location, the estate was linked with footpaths through Denaby and North Cliff Crags and to Denaby Main and in 1929 the Mexborough & Swinton trolleybus was extended to a new terminus in front of Wembley Avenue. Around 1930, a rather grand brick building was built forming an entrance feature to the estate complete with a central arch and separate gentleman and ladies waiting room, public toilets and a clock. This served as a waiting room for passengers at the trolleybus terminus and was occasionally known as the Wembley Arch but commonly referred to as the clock. The structure was demolished in the 1960s.

To the south of Old Road, Conisbrough Urban District Council began to build their first council estate and these homes were available to anyone, not just miners. Between 1923 and 1930 they provided 352 houses constructed in blocks of 2, 4 and 6 and of a similar standard to those provided by the colliery company to the north of Old Road, but this time with bathrooms provided upstairs. The Council laid out the streets of Daylands Avenue, Hamelin Road, Conan Road, Lewes Road, Prior Road, and St Peter's Road. St Peter's Road was named after St Peter's Church in Conisbrough whilst Lewes Road and Prior Road reflected the Cluniac Priory of Lewes in Sussex, which had been established by William de Warenne of Conisbrough Castle. Hamelin Street was named after Hamelin Plantagenet who first started the construction of the castle in 1159, whilst Conan Road also reflected the influence of the Norman Conquest, possibly named after Conan II of Renes, the Duke of Brittany.

The Avenues and council estate became known as Conanby, although the derivation of the name remains uncertain. Some believe it reflects a portmanteau word, taking the 'Con' from Conisbrough and the 'aby' from Denaby. Others have said that the names Conan (and Daylands) were from early Conisbrough Urban District councillors although records have so far proved fruitless. Maybe the name was derived from Conan Road (which formed the main entrance into the council estate) and hence was named after Conan II of Renes, the Duke of Brittany. In 1931, the Barnsley Brewery opened a new pub on Old Road to serve the new housing developments and this was named Lord Conyers Hotel, after the owner of the manor of Conisbrough, Sackville George Pelham, formerly Earl of Yarbrough and who became Lord Conyers from 1926.

Other post 1920 housing projects in Denaby Main were small in number, but included the construction in 1933 of the first private housing when 23 detached and semi-detached properties were built on land in Wheatley Street, Hickleton

Street and Church Walk, belonging to the Denaby Main Industrial & Co-operative Society. In 1938, Conisbrough Urban District Council provided 16 houses in Church Road and, following the Second World War, this project was completed with the provision of 6 of Sir Edwin Airey's prefabricated concrete houses in 1948. The council also provided the first pensioners bungalows in 1958 with the construction of properties in Shephard Close with more following in 1960 when All Saints Square was laid out in the former All Saints Vicarage gardens. During the 1960s, at North Cliff, the council erected eleven blocks of low rise flats.

Following the end of the Second World War there were extensive housing developments in Conisbrough. In 1948, Conisbrough Urban District Council provided 38 Airey houses in Old Road and Harthill Road whilst in 1949 they constructed 96 properties in blocks of 2 and 4 along the southern side of Cadeby Avenue, and laid out Wortley Avenue and Thirlwall Avenue, the latter named after Henry Thirlwall, the council's surveyor.

This 1950s Postcard by an anonymous photographer of Chestnut Grove is captioned 'Concrete Canyon'. The Coal Industry Housing Association houses were all finished with a grey concrete exterior, hence the area gained the name 'Concrete Canyon'. On completion, many Scottish families moved into this area.

In 1952, the National Coal Board established the Coal Industry Housing Association with the aim of providing 24,000 houses in areas suffering from manpower deficiency, mostly in the coalfields of Yorkshire and East Midlands, and a scheme was implemented to encourage miners and their families to move to the region from Scotland and the North East of England where their collieries were facing exhaustion of their reserves. Consequently the Coal Industry Housing Association constructed the Groves Estate from 1953 to 1955, laying out a development of 370 houses in pairs and blocks of 4, together with a parade of shops and a new social club, called the Groves Social Club. All the streets on the Groves Estates were named after different trees followed by the suffix Grove.

Further Conisbrough Urban District Council estates were provided in the 1950s and 1960s with the opening of an extension to the Groves estate and the construction of the Ellershaw estate. Additional housing was provided to the west of the Avenues estate with the construction of Locksley, Cedar, Scott and Oldfield Avenues. Finally the old windmill near Clifton Hill on the Doncaster side of Conisbrough was purchased from Frederick Montagu and subsequently demolished and the site used for the building of the Windmill Estate. In what proved to be an unsightly move, blocks of low rise flats were built adjacent to Conisbrough Castle, although these have since been demolished.

Maltby Street undergoing demolition in 1970 with the houses of Braithwell Street beyond awaiting a similar fate. The tower of the Large Hall School on Rossington Street can be seen top right. The demolition caused some bitterness from members of the community as neighbours who had lived together for many years were then rehoused in different parts of the new village. Note the pavement, constructed out of brick blocks engraved with a diamond pattern (Conisbrough & Denaby Main Heritage Group Collection).

Towards the end of the 1960s the local council decided that the old village of Denaby Main was no longer fit for purpose and they initiated a scheme to demolish the entire village and replace it with a new settlement. This project started in 1967 with the demolition of the original houses constructed during Phase 1 and continued throughout the 1970s working eastwards until all of the 1,727 colliery houses belonging to the NCB and constructed during Phases 1 to 6 plus the blocks of shops on Doncaster Road had been cleared. As demolition took place, construction of a new village commenced in its wake with ownership of the new properties transferring from the NCB to the local authority. The new settlement, built with an entirely different street pattern, was provided with various houses, bungalows, community centres and shopping facilities and a new Denaby Main Institute opened in 1972. In 1974, Conisbrough Urban District Council was absorbed by the newly established Doncaster Metropolitan Borough Council which took over the project, expanding the building area over land previously occupied by the allotments. In the early 1980s the council completed the project with the building of Harrogate Drive and a new road called Hill Top Road was constructed to link the new village with Conanby where the council was providing additional housing in the Knaresborough Road area.

The yearlong national Miner's Strike during 1984/5 undertaken in the defence of jobs brought the return of hardship to the region as Cadeby Main Colliery was one of 70 collieries earmarked for closure by the National Coal Board. Although there weren't the civil disturbances and police presence to the extent as seen at neighbouring colliery villages, the National Union of Mineworkers was instrumental in organising strike pay and picket lines and soup kitchens were provided by various women's support groups. After a year on strike and fighting a bitter contest against a Government who seemed determined to beat the miners at any cost, the men reluctantly returned to work. The National Union of Mineworkers was subsequently proved right when many of the country's remaining collieries were closed down at an alarming rate and, within two years of the strike ending, Cadeby Main Colliery would close after providing 98 years of coal production.

Today very little sign of the two pits and the original colliery village survives apart from some of the later stages of housing provided for deputies, officials and management in Wheatley Street, Tickhill Street, Tickhill Square and Buckingham Road, and with changing habits and a different environment, many of the clubs and societies have closed down or operate with reduced membership. The Reresby Arms was demolished and the Denaby Main hotel, once criticised by the *Christian Budget* for its excessive sale of alcohol, has become an Indian Restaurant. However, despite the near disappearance of the two pits and the original mining village, the local community remains and can be very proud of its contribution towards the industrial success of the country.

An atmospheric photograph taken through the central arch of the architectural feature known informally as 'the Clock' on Welfare Avenue, Conanby, as captured on 29th December 1960 by Peter Bagshawe. Through the arch can be seen a vehicle belonging to the Mexborough & Swinton Traction Company, a Sunbeam F4 with 32 seat bodywork by the Brush Electrical Engineering Company. This trolleybus was delivered in 1950, numbered 37 in the fleet and registered JWW 375. It is about to depart for its destination of Manvers Main Colliery travelling via Conisbrough, Denaby and Mexborough. Note the remains of the Conisborough Urban District Council election poster on the left. (Peter Bagshawe)

On Sunday 9th July 2012, a memorial was unveiled in Denaby Cemetery by 94 year old Irene Newton of Weston-Super-Mare. Irene's grandfather was amongst the 91 men and boys who died following the two explosions at Cadeby Main Colliery 100 years earlier. The service was attended by the local MP Caroline Flint, members of the community and several of the descendants of the disaster who laid wreaths. At 11am, the time of the second explosion, church bells in the district were rung 91 times in memory of the victims. In the north-eastern corner of the cemetery, near the Miners Welfare, are the graves of several of the men and boys who died in the disaster and nearby is the grave of William Henry Chambers, the managing director of the colliery company.

A note on the illustrations

Several of the illustrations in this book are taken from postcards that were published by photographers who toured the region during the period 1910-1930. Although no one photographer comprehensively captured the area (views of the back streets of Denaby remain elusive), between them they produced an incredible body of work. These photographers include:

John Crowther-Cox of Rotherham who recorded numerous views of Conisbrough and Denaby Main and in 1906/7 produced a marvellous series showing the construction of the Dearne Valley Railway Viaduct.

Edgar Leonard Scrivens (ELS) who visited Denaby in 1930 producing a small set of postcards depicting the township.

Regina Press Photographers of Doncaster who recorded a series of views of the Cadeby Pit Disaster and the 1912 National Strike.

James Simonton & Sons (JS&S) of Balby who visited Denaby in 1915 and later returned during the interwar period and the early 1950s, capturing the village's transformation during these years.

Walter Roelich, a Doncaster photographer who later formed the Doncaster Rotophoto Company with Charles Jamson and who produced a series of 60 Denaby Main postcards around 1920.

R. J. Rossor, a local photographer from Conisbrough produced a fine collection of postcards around 1910.

A piece of polished coal produced as a souvenir of the discovery of the Barnsley seam at Cadeby Main Colliery on January 19th 1893. The piece is inscribed on the base 'T Crabtree', and was passed down through the generations into the safe keeping of Margaret Briggs. (Reproduced by permission of Margaret's daughter Julie Knight).

Glossary

Barnsley Seam. A highly prized seam of coal up to 10 feet thick within the Coal Measures of South Yorkshire which is only found at the surface near the town of Barnsley but lies buried at depth in the Doncaster area.

Bunker. A large container used for the storage of coal before the coal can be treated in the screens and washery of a coal preparation plant.

Cage. A steel structure used to transport men or coal filled tubs up and down the shafts. Some cages had two decks. The cage was attached by a steel rope to the winding engine.

Cannel. A type of bituminous coal.

Coal Measures. A thick sequence of rocks and strata which consists of sandstones, shales, clays and coal seams. The coal measures of Yorkshire contain around 30 different coal seams.

Coal Preparation Plant. A building where the treatment of coal is undertaken prior to dispatch, usually containing screens, washery and a conveyor leading to a rapid loading bunker.

Coalfield (Exposed & Concealed). An area of land above coal measure rocks. A coalfield may be "exposed", i.e. the coal measures are found at the surface, or "concealed" where they are hidden at greater depths beneath younger rocks. Doncaster is situated on a concealed coalfield where the coal measures are buried beneath Magnesian Limestone and Bunter Sandstones.

Debenture. A type of long term loan, often used by companies to raise money and paid back at a fixed rate of interest.

Drift. A sloping tunnel connecting coal seams to the base of the shafts or to the surface.

Fault. A geological fracture resulting from the upward or downward movement of rock strata.

Gob. The area left following removal of a coal seam. It is supported with waste material or allowed to collapse in a controlled way.

Headgear. A structure of wooden, steel lattice or reinforced concrete construction situated above the shafts and used to support the winding wheels.

Heapstead. A structure located beneath the headgear providing a covered means of transport for coal exiting the shafts via filled tubs enabling transport to the nearby screens buildings.

Longwall Mining. A method of coal working in which coal is mined from a long coal face. The coal face connects two tunnels which lead back to the base of the shafts. The coalface thus advances away from the shafts leaving an area of gob behind. This method was later replaced by retreat mining.

Main. A suffix used mainly in South Yorkshire to denote those collieries which mined the largest or main seam from the coal measures, i.e. the Barnsley Seam
Pillar and Stall Mining. A method of coal working where coal was extracted from areas known as stalls leaving pillars of coal to support the surface. Largely replaced with longwall mining due to the advance in technology in the 19th Century.
Pit. A local term for a coal mine or colliery
Rapid Loading Bunker. A large bunker containing many tons of coal which is dropped into railway wagons passing beneath the structure.
Retreat Mining. The most economical method in mining in which roadways are driven out to the extremity of the royalty so that a coal face can then be worked back towards the shaft bottom. Largely superseded longwall mining in the 1950s/1960s.
Rake. A group of railway coaches or wagons all coupled together.
Roadways. Underground tunnels leading from the bottom of the shaft to the coal faces.
Royalty. An area of land beneath which coal can be extracted by paying a fee or royalty on every ton produced to the landowner.
Screens. A building containing numerous devices for sorting individual lumps of coal by size or weight.
Shafts. A vertical tunnel from the surface to the coal seam through which the coal is raised and men and materials can access the workings. Following a mining disaster at Hartley Colliery in County Durham each colliery was required to have two shafts, downcast and upcast, to aid escape in the event of an accident. Air was pumped through the downcast shaft to ventilate the workings and then drawn out of the colliery via the upcast shaft.
Shaft Pillar. An area of coal left intact in order to support the colliery's surface buildings and thus protect them from the effects of subsidence. Some coal was removed from the shaft pillar to form roadways or tunnels to access the underground workings.
Sinking. The process of tunnelling vertically downwards from the surface to the coal seam in order to construct a shaft, usually undertaken by workers called sinkers who specialised in this highly skilled but dangerous work.
Skip Winding. A method of winding coal up a shaft by the use of a large capacity metal container or skip. A more economical way of transport than that previously used when individual coal filled tubs were brought to the surface in a cage.
Staithes. A landing stage for the loading of cargo into boats.
Tubbing. A waterproof casing, usually of iron, inserted into a shaft as it was sunk in order to keep back water and soft sediments.
Tubs. Small wagons used to transport coal underground, usually hauled by pit ponies.
Tumblers. Machinery for screening and sorting coal.
Washery. A surface plant building for dealing with the cleaning and washing of coal.
Wayleave. A royalty paid to the owner of the land on which the colliery is situated.
Winding Engine. An engine, initially steam driven but later powered by electricity, used to raise the cages up and down the colliery shafts.

Bibliography

Abercrombie, P. and Johnson, T. H. (1922). The Doncaster Regional Planning Scheme, Hodder & Stoughton Ltd, London.
Anon, (nd c1970s?). Coal and Colliers - a profile of Denaby in 1871. (Typed notes in Doncaster Archives)
Anon, (1899). Roads to Ruins: Betting and Gambling, Part IV, The Worst Village in England, Christian Budget, November 8th 1899, p531-532.
Bailey, C. (2007). Black Diamonds, the rise and fall of an English Dynasty. Penguin Books, London.
Barker, C. (2008). Mexborough & Swinton Trolleybuses, Middleton Press, Midhurst.
Barnett, A. L. (1984). The Railways of the South Yorkshire Coalfield from 1880. RCTS Publishing, Devon.
Benson, J. & Neville, R. G. (Eds, 1976). Studies in the Yorkshire Coal Industry, Manchester University Press.
Colliery Guardian (1927). The Colliery Year Book & Coal Trades Directory. Louis Cassier Publishing, London.
Booth, A. J. (1990). A railway history of Denaby and Cadeby Collieries, Industrial Railway Society, Bridlington.
Elliott, B, (Ed, 1999). Aspects of Doncaster, Discovering Local History Volume 2. Wharncliffe Publishing, Barnsley
Elliott, B. (2009). South Yorkshire Mining Disasters Vol II: The Twentieth Century. Wharncliffe Publishing, Barnsley.

Denaby & Cadeby Main Miners Memorial Chapel (1987). Booklet issued at the dedication of the chapel.
Gwatkin, J. (1990). A photographic record of the old village of Denaby Main. Privately Published.
Gwatkin. J. (1990). Postscript to a photographic record of the old village of Denaby Main. Privately Published.
Gwatkin, J. & Davies, P. (2012). Some aspects of Cadeby Main Colliery. Cadeby Main Memorial Group, Denaby.
Hill, A. (2001). The South Yorkshire Coalfield, a history and development. Tempus Publishing, Stroud.
Howells, S. (2015). Coal owner into Ship owner: Denaby and Cadeby. In Ships in Focus Record 61, July 2015. Ships in Focus Publications, London.
Jones, M. (1999). Denaby Main: the development of a South Yorkshire Mining Village. *In Elliott (1999) qv, p123-144.*
MacFarlane, J. E. (1976). Denaby Main: A South Yorkshire mining village. *In Benson & Neville (1976), qv, p109-144.*
MacFarlane, J. E. (1987). The Bag Muck Strike Denaby Main, 1902-1903. Doncaster Library Service.
Maye, R. A. (1986). St Alban's Parish Church, Denaby. Doncaster Library Service.
McLister, G. (1988). Cadeby, the end of an era. Doncaster Library Service.
Modern Methods of Coal Production and Shipment (no date c1928). Yorkshire Amalgamated Collieries Ltd.
Pearson, B. (1997). History of Conisbrough and Denaby. Privately Published.
Tomlinson, J (1879). From Doncaster into Hallamshire. Brook White & Hatfield, Doncaster.
Ward, J. T. (1976). West Riding landowners and mining in the nineteenth century. In Benson & Neville (1976) qv, p45-65.

Websites (All links correct at the time of publication)

http://www.cmhrc.co.uk/site/home/index.html The Coal Mining History Resource Centre, maintained by Raleys Solicitors includes a database of deaths and accidents at British Collieries.
https://www.facebook.com/groups/dearnevalleyinoldphotos. Photographic group, admin Andrew McGarrigle.
http://www.genealogy.com/ftm/p/o/p/Owen-James-Pope/WEBSITE-0001/UHP-0440.html. Contains detailed biographical information on the Pope family.
http://keithsphotos.webs.com/. An extensive photographic database of the area, complied by Keith Butcher.
http://www.conisbroughheritage.co.uk/. The website of the Conisbrough & Denaby Main Local Heritage Group